THE ULTIMATE COOKBOOK FOR TEEN CHEFS

1000 Days of Easy Step-by-step Recipes and Essential Techniques to Inspire Young Cooks|Full Color Pictures Version

FRANCISCA W. CHILDS

Table of Contents

Introduction

Dear Teen Chef,

Y ou'll be happy to know that you are not alone in your quest for nourishment. If you're reading this, it means that you're curious about cooking, and who knows, maybe you're already coming up with your recipes. Just as there is a science to cooking, there is also a science to writing cookbooks: How to organize information about the topic; how to organize a recipe into its various parts; how to make all of this clear and easy to follow; how to test the recipes so that they work; and much more. This book will give you the basics of understanding recipes and cooking. If you have ever wanted to cook like a gourmet chef and impress friends and family with your culinary skills, this book is for you. It promises to teach the secrets to classic recipes in easy steps with simple directions and helpful techniques. Whether you are seven or seventy, this handbook will guide you through the process.

Terminology

Culinary Arts: Culinary arts are the practical skills needed to prepare food safely and skillfully in a commercial kitchen environment. The term includes, but is not limited to, cooking; baking; canning; storing; freezing; producing; serving (e.g., waiting for staff); and decorating (e.g., garnishing).

Prep: is to prepare equipment and ingredients as per the recipe.

Drippings: liquid left after roasting meat.

Pare: remove the outer layer of vegetables and fruits using a peeler.

Whip: incorporate air bubbles in creams or protein-rich liquids.

Deglaze: add a liquid such as broth to a hot pan after cooking meat to pick up the concentrated flavors in the pan.

Roux: a thickener made of equal parts fat and flour that is slowly cooked.

Broil: to cook food directly under the heat source

Cooking Equipment

TOOLS & UTENSILS

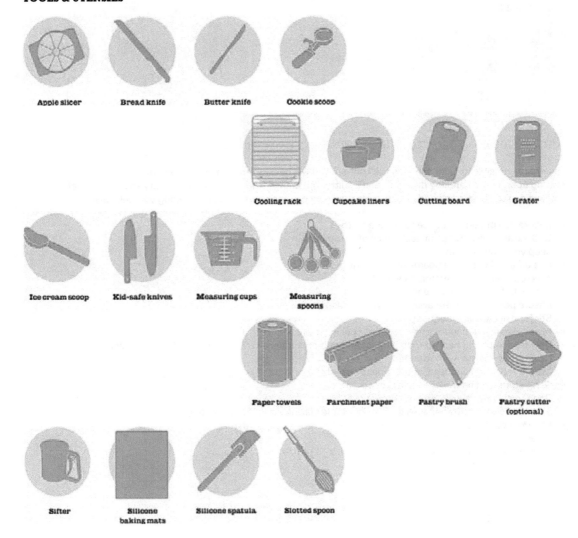

Apple slicer   Bread knife   Butter knife   Cookie scoop

Cooling rack   Cupcake liners   Cutting board   Grater

Ice cream scoop   Kid-safe knives   Measuring cups   Measuring spoons

Paper towels   Parchment paper   Pastry brush   Pastry cutter (optional)

Sifter   Silicone baking mats   Silicone spatula   Slotted spoon

Vegetable peeler	Whisk	Wooden mixing spoons (optional)	Zester

COOKWARE & BAKEWARE

Baking pan (8-by-8-inch, 9-by-9-inch, and 9-by-13-inch)	Baking sheet (two 9-by-13-inch)	Bundt pan	Cake pan (8-inch and 9-inch [round])	Muffin pan (two 12-cup)	Skillet (including cast iron)

APPLIANCES

Food processor	Stand mixer with paddle attachment and dough hook or electric beaters

Kitchen Safety Measures you Should Understand

You are responsible for your safety in the kitchen. You will be cooking with hot ingredients, using sharp knives and cutting boards, and handling raw meat and poultry. You should have basic kitchen safety knowledge that will help you avoid injury to yourself and others. Here are some common sense tips for keeping yourself safe:

- Ensure you put on your shoes and safe clothes.
- Understand the purpose of each piece of equipment in your kitchen.
- Keep your hands clean.
- Use different chopping boards for different foods.
- Keep cooked food away from raw food.
- Take your time with your cooking.
- Ensure pets and kids are away from your cooking area.
- Stir food away from your body
- Always keep your fingers away from hot cooking surfaces.
- Only try something new after consulting an adult or someone who knows what they are doing.
- Never leave the stove unattended.
- Keep the oven door closed, and the heat turned off.
- Don't store food on top of cabinets or counters.
- Don't use metal utensils on plastic pans.
- Store all knives on the same block or in the same place so they're easy to find.
- Keep knives sharpened and clean, with no rust or other signs of damage.
- Clean up spills in your kitchen.
- Have a fire extinguisher and know how to use it.
- Don't handle food when sick.

Chapter 2
Getting Ready to Cook

WHY DO YOU NEED TO READ AND UNDERSTAND YOUR RECIPE?

You need to understand the instructions to know the ingredients, how much of each one is needed, and how they should be combined. Reading through the instructions helps you understand what's actually happening as your dish cooks. It is worth quickly reading over the entire recipe before you start, so you have an idea of what's ahead. Knowing what needs to be done ahead of time will help ensure that nothing goes wrong during cooking (like forgetting to whisk something in with another ingredient) or when putting the finishing touches on a dish (like not knowing what kind of cheese is used in a particular pizza).

WHAT TO WEAR

While you're cooking, it's important that you stay comfortable and relaxed. That's why we recommend wearing comfortable clothing. If you're spending much time in the kitchen, invest in some safety gear: a pair of oven mitts, an apron, and some goggles to keep you from burning your hands or dropping hot pans on yourself. You should also prepare for any potential messes by wearing an old shirt or jacket that can be easily cleaned. If you want to look professional, try wearing a chef's hat or apron. This will make you look like an authority figure who knows what they are doing, which is exactly what you need in the kitchen! Try wearing jeans instead of pants so that your legs are covered up. If you need help getting ready for cooking, don't hesitate to ask for help—it's better than putting off making dinner until tomorrow night!

Recipes to try in the comfort of your home

- Breakfast recipes (Pumpkin Pancakes).
- Snacks, Sides, and Drinks (Corn Casserole).
- Meat and Seafood (Easy Beef Stroganoff).
- Sauces and Dips (Mustard Sauce).
- Meatless recipes (One-pot Zucchini Mushroom Pasta).
- Desserts (Apple Spice Cake).

What Are the Cooking Methods?

Teenagers are known for their impulsive nature and poor decision-making skills. But they can still cook! A new age of chefs is upon us, and the best way to get your teen started is to start with simple recipes that they can follow without much supervision. When teaching your child how to cook, it's important to remember that they're still learning to make decisions. This means you should always ensure they're using safe ingredients, following instructions closely, and not over-cooking their food. A few cooking methods are especially good for teens, such as baking, roasting, and grilling. These are great because they require fewer ingredients and don't require much cleanup. Having an oven that is always ready to go means that you don't have to worry about having the right tools or ingredients. It's also convenient because it doesn't require any cleanup—power down the appliance and set it aside once you're done with it.

BAKING

Baking requires less prep time than other cooking methods. You can prepare your ingredients ahead of time while they're still fresh, which means less time spent in the kitchen cleaning up. Baking also doesn't require any special tools or ingredients.

ROASTING

Roasting is quick and easy. You can roast almost anything in an oven, including chicken breasts and vegetables like potatoes and carrots! Roasting also requires little preparation before cooking begins—you only need oil and seasonings on hand!

GRILLING

Grilling requires little preparation before cooking begins—heat your grill to medium heat.

STEAMING

This is cooking food using steam. You can use a steamer or a wok to steam your food. It doesn't require a lot of time or equipment to steam. Some of the best steamed foods include vegetables, eggs, fish, and shellfish.

BRAISING

Braising is a cooking technique that involves cooking food in liquid, usually by browning in oil or fat.

SAUTEING

Sauteing is a cooking technique that involves cooking food in a small amount of oil or fat over moderate heat. The food is cooked by swirling the pan, stirring frequently, and adding more oil or fat to prevent sticking.

FRYING

Frying is cooking food in hot fat or oil, typically in a shallow pan. In deep-frying, food is completely immersed in a deeper vessel of hot oil.

OTHER COOKING METHODS INCLUDE:

- Boiling
- Broiling
- Poaching
- Stewing
- Searing
- Blanching

How to Be A Better Chef

You can be a better chef. It's not easy, but it is doable. You need to understand the fundamentals of cooking to reach your potential as a young chef. What does this mean? Well, the fundamentals include cutting ingredients into uniform shapes, properly seasoning your food, and properly cooking meats and vegetables in different ways to bring out their unique flavors.

Don't reinvent the wheel—there are already tons of great recipes! Instead of trying to reinvent the wheel, use one of these tried-and-true methods: googling it (or looking up a website) or asking someone who knows what they're doing (like your parents) for advice on where to start.

Make sure your ingredients are fresh—it might seem like a small thing, but if you don't use high-quality ingredients, your meal will not have the quality it needs! Try using organic spices whenever possible; they cost more than conventional ones, but they taste better too!

Be flexible—if something doesn't work out immediately, don't be afraid to try again.

Tips for Success

Teen chefs are an important part of society. They're the future of our culinary world, and we must give them the tools to succeed in the kitchen. This cookbook is designed to help you get started on your path as a teen chef. Getting started can be a challenge. There are so many things to learn, and it can take time to figure out where to start. Here are some tips for making the most of your time in the kitchen:

- Keep track of what you learned. Write down notes about what you did and how it went. This will help you remember all the steps you took and what worked well or not so well.
- Make friends with other teens who love cooking! You'll find that they have lots of helpful advice and stories from their own experiences with cooking, which will help you when you're trying new things too!
- Be patient with yourself and your skills—you'll get there! Remember that learning takes time, but every little bit of progress counts!
- Keep an inventory of the ingredients and tools you use every time you cook. If something breaks or gets lost, it'll be easier to remember to replace it. You'll also prevent waste by not buying ingredients you already have.
- Don't spend too much time prepping your food before cooking it—the shorter the prep time, the better! If possible, try using ingredients that require little or no prep work before cooking them.
- Make sure that everything in your fridge is labeled with what is inside it and how long it will last (i.e., "chicken" instead of "breast" or "meatballs" instead of "turkey"). This will help others find what they're looking for, and it will help you prevent having to throw out old food.
- Find your comfort zone. If you're getting into cooking for the first time, you probably need help figuring out how to start. Take it one step at a time, and don't rush. Just find something that makes you feel comfortable and practice what you've learned until it becomes second nature.
- Keep learning! Keep reading about new techniques and recipes, even if you've mastered them.

Teen chefs are the next generation of culinary pioneers. They're not afraid to get their hands dirty, and they have a lot to say about what it takes to make great food. We're proud to be part of this movement, and we hope our cookbook will inspire you to create your recipes and share them with the world! We hope you've enjoyed reading our teen chefs' cookbook! We know it can be overwhelming to figure out what to cook for dinner every night or for a party, so we're glad we can make it easier. Now that you have a cookbook full of delicious food, it's time to share it with your friends and family! Happy cooking!

Chapter 3
Breakfast

Baked Eggs and Spinach in Sweet Potato Boats
Prep Time: 30 minutes | Cook Time: 1 hour 20 minutes | Serves 4

- 2 sweet potatoes, large
- Pepper and salt
- 1 tbsp butter
- 1 cup finely chopped baby spinach, packed
- 4 eggs

1. Preheat an oven to 400oF.
2. Bake sweet potatoes for about 45-60 minutes in the oven.
3. Halve each sweet potato and scoop most of its flesh out leaving a small flesh rim around the potato skin.
4. Season each half with pepper and salt.
5. Add butter cubes to each potato half then top with spinach. Season again with pepper and salt.
6. Break an egg carefully into each half.
7. Bake the potato halves in your preheated oven for about 15 minutes until the eggs cook to your liking.
8. Lastly, season once more with pepper and salt.
9. Serve and enjoy.

Savory Keto Breakfast Cookies
Prep Time: 10 minutes | Cook Time: 25 minutes | Serves 12

- 3 eggs, large
- 1-1/2 cups almond flour
- 1 tbsp baking powder
- 1 cup finely shredded cheddar cheese
- Black pepper
- 1/2 tbsp salt
- Optional
- 3 cooked bacon strips, crumbled
- 1 minced scallion

1. Preheat your oven to 350oF. Use parchment paper to line a baking sheet.
2. Place eggs, almond flour, baking powder, cheese, black pepper, and salt in a mixing bowl. Mix using a rubber spatula until stiff and combined.
3. Fold in bacon and scallions if using.
4. Divide the mixture into mounds and place on the lined baking sheet, about 12 in a batch, and then smooth the edges into a circular shape with slightly dampened fingers.
5. Flatten the mound tops until cookies of ¾ inch thick.
6. Bake the cookies on the oven middle rack for about 14-16 minutes until the edges are lightly golden and firm.
7. When done, remove from the oven and let cool for about 5 minutes.
8. Serve and enjoy!

Breakfast Burrito

Prep Time: 10 minutes | Cook Time: 1 minute 25 seconds | Serves 1

- 2 large eggs
- Salt
- Freshly ground black pepper
- 1 large (10-inch) whole-wheat flour tortilla
- ¼ cup precooked turkey sausage crumbles
- 1 to 2 tablespoons frozen diced bell pepper, thawed
- 1 tablespoon shredded cheese (Cheddar or mozzarella work well)

1. Following the recipe for Quick and Easy Scrambled Eggs, cook the eggs.
2. Place the tortilla on a clean work surface. Arrange the turkey sausage, bell pepper, scrambled eggs, and cheese on top.
3. To wrap into a burrito, fold the sides of the tortilla in toward the middle of the burrito, then carefully fold the bottom of the burrito around the eggs and meat, pulling gently toward you to create a tight roll, then roll up the rest of the way.
4. Place the burrito on a microwave-safe plate and microwave on high power for 25 seconds.

Simple Scrambled Eggs

Prep Time: 5 minutes | Cook Time: 5-10 minutes | Serves 4

- 6 to 8 eggs
- Kosher salt
- Freshly ground black pepper
- 4 tablespoons butter
- Flake salt, such as Maldon, for finishing

1. Crack the eggs into a small bowl, and whisk until frothy. Season with salt and pepper.
2. Melt the butter in a medium sauté pan over medium heat, and then turn the heat to low as the butter foams. Pour the eggs in and let sit for a few seconds.
3. Use a spatula to nudge and stir the eggs, scraping the bottom continuously as you move them around the pan to help prevent sticking. Use the spatula to push the eggs from center-out, and then scrape the pan edge, swirling the outermost eggs into the center. Keep doing this until the eggs begin to look like pudding and then form into dense, rich egg curds, about 4 minutes.
4. Remove the pan from the heat while the eggs are still a little loose; they will continue to cook on the way from the pan to your plate. Sprinkle with a little flake salt and pepper, and eat at once.

Cheesy Baked Eggs

Prep Time: 20 minutes | Cook Time: 30 minutes | Serves 1

- 1 tbsp softened butter
- 2 tbsp milk, half and half or cream
- 2 large eggs
- Pinch of black pepper
- Pinch of salt
- 2 tbsp cheddar cheese, shredded
- 1 tbsp parmesan cheese, grated

1. Preheat your oven to 400oF.
2. In the meantime, coat inside of an oven ramekin, 8-ounces, with butter.
3. Whisk milk and eggs in a bowl, small.
4. Stir in pepper, salt, and cheeses.
5. Pour the batter into the ramekin.
6. Bake for about 15-18 minutes until eggs are cooked through.
7. Let cool for about 5 minutes and serve.
8. Enjoy!

Pancakes with Chocolate-Banana Crunch

Prep Time: 25 minutes | Cook Time: 25 minutes | Serves 6-8

- For the pancakes
- 4 tablespoons unsalted butter
- 1½ cups all-purpose flour
- 3 tablespoons sugar
- 1½ teaspoons baking powder
- ½ teaspoon salt
- ¼ teaspoon baking soda
- 1 cup plus 2 tablespoons milk
- 1 large egg
- Cooking spray
- For the toppings
- 4 ounces semisweet chocolate
- 3 tablespoons heavy cream
- 2 tablespoons honey
- 1 banana, sliced
- Granola, for topping

1. Microwave the butter in a small microwave-safe bowl until melted.
2. Combine the flour, sugar, baking powder, salt and baking soda in a medium bowl and whisk to combine. Combine the milk, melted butter and egg in a separate medium bowl and whisk to combine. Add the milk mixture to the flour mixture and whisk until just combined (it's OK if there are some lumps).
3. Heat a large nonstick skillet or griddle over medium-low heat and coat with cooking spray. Pour in ¼ cup of the batter with a ladle or measuring cup for each pancake and cook until bubbly on top and golden on the bottom, about 4 minutes. Flip with a spatula and cook until golden on the other side, about 2 more minutes. Remove the pancakes and place on a plate.
4. Make the toppings: Carefully chop the chocolate with a chef's knife. Combine the chopped chocolate, heavy cream and honey in a small microwave-safe bowl. Microwave 30 seconds, then stir with a spoon. Continue to microwave, stirring every 30 seconds, until the sauce is smooth. Top the pancakes with the banana slices, chocolate sauce and granola.

Blueberry Blast Banana Bread
Prep Time: 20 minutes | Cook Time: 1 hour | Serves 12

- Butter, for greasing the pan
- 2 large eggs
- 1 cup ripe banana (about 2 medium bananas)
- 1 cup buttermilk
- ⅓ cup brown sugar
- ⅔ cup canola oil (you can use half oil plus half applesauce if you like)
- 2 cups whole-wheat flour
- 1 cup old-fashioned rolled oats
- 2 teaspoons baking powder
- 1 teaspoon ground cinnamon
- ½ teaspoon salt
- ¼ teaspoon baking soda
- 1 cup blueberries

1. Oil the pan, and preheat the oven. Use your fingers or a paper towel to spread butter all over the inside of the loaf pan. Preheat the oven to 375˚F.
2. Measure and stir together the wet ingredients. In a medium bowl, crack 1 egg. Remove any shells, and pour the egg into a large bowl. Repeat with the second egg. In another medium bowl, mash the bananas with a fork or a potato masher. Add the bananas to the large bowl with the eggs, and stir. Add the buttermilk, brown sugar, and oil, and whisk* until blended
3. Measure the dry ingredients, and mix all ingredients. In another large bowl, mix the flour, oats, baking powder, cinnamon, salt, and baking soda. Using a rubber spatula or wooden spoon, stir the flour mixture into the buttermilk mixture, mixing just until combined. Gently fold* in the blueberries. Pour the batter into the greased loaf pan.
4. Bake the bread. Bake for about 1 hour, or until the loaf is brown and a toothpick inserted into the center comes out clean. Cool in the pan for 15 minutes before cutting into slices and serving.

Microwave Frittata
Prep Time: 5 minutes | Cook Time: 5 minutes | Serves 1

- 2 large eggs
- 1 tablespoon milk
- ¼ cup shredded mozzarella cheese
- 2 tablespoons chopped tomato
- Kosher salt and freshly ground pepper

1. Combine the eggs and milk in a microwave-safe mug and lightly beat with a fork. Add the cheese and tomato, season with salt and pepper and stir until combined.
2. Microwave, stirring every 20 seconds with a spoon, until the eggs are just set, about 1 minute.

Waffle Egg-in-a-Hole

Prep Time: 15 minutes | Cook Time: 5 minutes | Serves 1

- 1 frozen waffle, thawed but not toasted
- 1 large egg
- 1 tablespoon unsalted butter
- Kosher salt and freshly ground pepper
- Pure maple syrup, for topping

1. Preheat the oven to 375°. Cut out a 2-inch hole from the center of the waffle with a cookie cutter or small drinking glass.
2. Crack the egg into a small bowl or ramekin. Melt the butter in a small ovenproof nonstick skillet over medium heat. Add the waffle and cook until toasted on the bottom, 2 to 3 minutes. Flip with a spatula. Carefully pour the egg into the hole in the waffle and season with salt and pepper. Cook until the egg white starts to set, about 2 minutes.
3. Carefully put the skillet in the oven and bake until the egg white is set but the yolk is still a little runny, about 4 minutes. Remove the skillet from the oven with oven mitts and remove the waffle to a plate with the spatula. Top with maple syrup.

Breakfast Burrito Bar

Prep Time: 10 minutes | Cook Time: 12 minutes | Serves 4

- 4 to 8 whole-grain (8- or 10-inch) tortillas
- 6 to 8 eggs, scrambled
- 2 cups canned black beans, drained and rinsed
- 3 strips cooked bacon, crumbled
- 1 cup Greek yogurt or sour cream
- 1 cup bite-size cilantro sprigs
- 1½ cups Salsa Fresca (here)
- ½ cup orange, red, or green bell peppers, diced
- 1½ cups shredded sharp Cheddar or Monterey Jack cheese
- 1½ cups diced avocado or No-Nonsense Guacamole (here)
- Sriracha or Cholula hot sauce, for garnish

1. Preheat the oven to 375°F.
2. Warm the tortillas.
3. Wrap a stack of 4 tortillas in aluminum foil and warm for 5 to 10 minutes. If you are preparing 8 tortillas, make 2 wrapped bundles. Wrap the warmed foil bundles in a dish towel to keep them toasty.
4. Serve the fillings and toppings in festive, colorful bowls. Arrange them together on the table or counter, along with the towel-wrapped tortillas, and allow your guests to assemble their own burrito creations.

Peanut Butter Banana Wafflewich

Prep Time: 10 minutes | Cook Time: 2 minutes | Serves 1

- 2 frozen whole-grain waffles
- 1 small banana
- 1 to 2 tablespoons smooth peanut butter or sunflower seed butter
- Honey, for drizzling

1. Put the waffles into a toaster. Toast for about 1 ½ minutes until lightly browned.
2. Peel the banana, then place it onto your cutting board and cut it into bite-size pieces.
3. Spread the peanut butter onto one of the toasted waffles. Arrange the banana pieces on top of the peanut butter. Drizzle with honey, then cover with the other waffle to make a sandwich.

Glazed French Toast Muffins

Prep Time: 15 minutes | Cook Time: 15 minutes | Serves 6

- Nonstick cooking spray
- 2 large eggs
- 2 tablespoons plus 1 teaspoon milk, divided
- 1 tablespoon granulated sugar
- ½ teaspoon ground cinnamon
- ½ teaspoon vanilla extract
- 4 slices cinnamon-raisin bread
- ¼ cup powdered sugar

1. Preheat the oven to 350°F.
2. Generously coat a 6-cup muffin pan with cooking spray, or line it with paper liners.
3. Crack the eggs into a medium bowl. Add 2 tablespoons of milk, the granulated sugar, cinnamon, and vanilla. Stir well to blend.
4. Place the bread slices on a cutting board and cut each into thirds, both horizontally and vertically, to make bread cubes, or tear the bread into bite-size chunks.
5. Stir the bread cubes into the egg mixture, taking care to coat all the bread.
6. Evenly divide the bread cube mixture among the prepared muffin cups. Gently press the bread down with the back of a spoon.
7. Transfer the pan to the preheated oven and bake for 15 minutes, or until golden brown. Using oven mitts, remove the pan from the oven.
8. Meanwhile, in a small bowl, stir together the powdered sugar and the remaining 1 teaspoon of milk. Pour the glaze over the warm muffins in the muffin pan.
9. French toast muffins are best enjoyed warm. To reheat, simply microwave them on high power for 45 seconds, or until warmed.

Savory Sausage Hash

Prep Time: 15 minutes | Cook Time: 15 minutes | Serves 4

- 2 tablespoons olive oil, divided
- 1 onion, finely chopped
- 3 Yukon gold potatoes, scrubbed and diced into ½-inch cubes
- 1 pound hot or Italian pork sausage, casings removed
- 2 garlic cloves, finely grated
- 1 small jalapeño, cored and seeded, finely chopped
- 2 tablespoons minced fresh rosemary
- 1 teaspoon dried smoked paprika
- Sea salt
- Freshly ground black pepper

1. Cook the onion and potatoes.
2. Place a large skillet over medium heat, and add 1 tablespoon of olive oil when the pan is hot. Add the onion and sauté for 5 minutes, or until they become translucent, stirring occasionally. Add the potatoes and the remaining 1 tablespoon of olive oil, and stir to incorporate. Sauté the mixture for another 5 minutes, stirring only a few times during this step so the potatoes can form a nice crust.
3. Add the sausage, garlic, and jalapeño, and brown the meat, crumbling it into smaller pieces with the edge of a wooden spoon. Add the rosemary and paprika, and season with salt and pepper. Stirring occasionally, lower the heat if needed as you cook the mixture, until the potatoes become crispy and fork tender and the meat is browned all over.
4. Serve from the skillet on a trivet at the table.

Bunny Pancakes

Prep Time: 15 minutes | Cook Time: 40 minutes | Serves 8

- 1¼ to 1½ cups milk, plus more if needed
- 2 tablespoons canola oil or olive oil, plus more for greasing the pan
- 1 tablespoon honey
- 1 teaspoon vanilla extract
- 2 eggs
- 1½ cups oat flour or whole-wheat flour
- 2 teaspoons baking powder
- ½ teaspoon baking soda
- ½ teaspoon salt
- 1 cup blueberries
- 2 tablespoons slivered almonds
- Butter, for serving
- Maple syrup (for serving, optional)
- Heavy cream (for serving, optional, see Make It Your Own here)

1. Measure and mix the wet ingredients. In a large bowl, combine the milk, oil, honey, and vanilla and stir together. In a medium bowl, crack 1 egg. Remove any shells, and pour the egg into the large bowl with the milk mixture. Repeat with the second egg and whisk* until the mixture is smooth.
2. Measure and mix the dry ingredients, and combine with wet ingredients. In another large bowl, mix the flour, baking powder, baking soda, and salt. Using a wooden spoon, gently stir the wet ingredients into the flour mixture until combined.
3. Oil the pan, and turn on the stove. Use a paper towel to rub oil into the bottom of a large skillet or pan. Place the skillet on the stove top, and heat over medium-low heat.
4. Cook the pancakes. Pour about ¼ cup of batter onto the skillet for each pancake. If the batter is too thick, stir in a little milk in the batter to thin. Cook until bubbly on top and golden on the bottom, about 4 minutes. Flip using a spatula, and cook until golden on the bottom, about 2 more minutes. Repeat with the remaining batter.
5. Make your bunnies! Make two bunny ears by cutting two sections off the edges of a pancake with a butter knife or make two long and skinny pancakes. Make cheeks with two smaller pancakes. Place bunny ears on top of a whole pancake, add blueberries for the eyes and nose, the two smaller pancakes for cheeks, and slivered almonds for whiskers.

Green Hulk Smoothie

Prep Time: 5 minutes | Cook Time: 10 minutes | Serves 1

- 1 cup fresh spinach
- 1 cup whole milk or non-dairy alternative
- 2 tablespoons honey (or to taste)
- 1 frozen banana

1. Rinse the spinach. Place the spinach in the colander and rinse it in the sink. Let it drain before completing step 3.
2. Combine the milk and honey. Pour the milk and honey into the blender.
3. Add the remaining ingredients. Add the banana and spinach to the blender.
4. Blend until completely smooth.
5. Serve. Pour the smoothie into a cup and enjoy!

Granola With Walnut and Raisins

Prep Time: 10 minutes | Cook Time: 25 minutes | Serves 12

- 3 cups old-fashioned oats
- 1/3 cup chopped walnuts
- 1/3 cup raw pumpkin seeds
- ¼ cup raw wheat germ
- ¼ cup flaked, sweetened coconut
- 1 Tbsp canola oil
- 1 tsp ground cinnamon
- ¼ tsp salt
- Grated zest of 1 orange
- ½ cup raisins

1. Preheat oven to 300°F. Spray a 10½" × 15½" jelly-roll pan with nonstick spray.
2. Mix all ingredients except raisins in a medium bowl. Transfer mixture into the prepared baking pan and spread evenly.
3. Bake for about 25 minutes. Add raisins and let cool in the pan on a wire rack.

Peach Melba Breakfast Pops

Prep Time: 10 minutes | Cook Time: 10 minutes plus 8 hours freezing time| Serves 6

- 2/3 cup vanilla Greek yogurt
- 2 tablespoons honey
- 2 small ripe peaches, chopped (about 1½ cups)
- ¼ cup raspberries halved
- ½ cup granola

1. Preparing the Ingredients. In a blender, combine yogurt, honey, and three-fourths of peaches until the mixture is smooth. Distribute raspberries and remaining peaches among 6 to 8 ice pop molds.
2. Fill each mold with about ¼ cup yogurt mixture, tapping to distribute, leaving ½ inch unfilled. Top with granola; pack granola tightly into yogurt until yogurt reaches the top of the mold.
3. Freeze for 6 to 8 hours or until solid.

Chapter 4
Poultry

Citrus Chicken Wings

Prep Time: 5 minutes | Cook Time: 24 minutes | Serves 10

- 2 pounds (907 g) chicken wings
- 4½ teaspoons salt-free lemon pepper seasoning
- 1½ teaspoons baking powder
- 1½ teaspoons kosher salt

1. In a large bowl, toss together all the ingredients until well coated. Place the wings on the sheet pan, making sure they don't crowd each other too much.
2. Select Air Fry. Set Air Fryer temperature to 375°F (190°C) and set time to 24 minutes. Press Start to begin preheating.
3. Once preheated, slide the pan into the oven.
4. After 12 minutes, remove the pan from the oven. Use tongs to turn the wings over. Rotate the pan and return the pan to the oven to continue cooking.
5. When cooking is complete, the wings should be dark golden brown and a bit charred in places. Remove the pan from the oven and let rest for 5 minutes before serving.

Chicken Enchilada Street Fries

Prep Time: 5 minutes | Cook Time: 20 minutes | Serves 2

- 2 ounces frozen French fries
- 1 cup shredded cooked chicken
- ½ cup canned red enchilada sauce
- ¼ cup sour cream
- 2 teaspoons milk
- ¼ cup canned black beans
- ¼ cup canned corn
- 1 red onion
- ½ cup shredded Cheddar cheese
- 1 lime wedge

1. Preheat the oven according to the fry package's directions, usually around 425°F. Line a small rimmed baking sheet with aluminum foil.
2. Place the fries on the prepared baking sheet and bake according to the package directions, usually about 20 minutes, or until crispy. Remove from the oven, leaving the oven on.
3. In a small bowl, combine the cooked chicken and enchilada sauce. Put the sour cream and milk in another small bowl. Stir to combine.
4. Drain the black beans and corn in a strainer, then rinse with cold water.
5. To finely dice the onion, start by cutting the onion in half from root to tip. Peel off the papery outside layer and a layer of onion underneath that. For each onion half, cut off the tip of the onion, but leave the root end intact. Cut each onion half in half again from root to tip. Place an onion quarter, flat-side down, on a cutting board. Make several vertical cuts from end to end, being careful not to cut through the root end. Flip the onion quarter onto the other flat side and repeat the vertical cuts, again being careful not to cut through the root end. Then cut the onion crosswise into small, even dice—the pieces should just fall off the knife ready to go. Set aside 2 tablespoons and store any leftover onion.
6. Switch the oven to broil.
7. Top the fries with the chicken mixture and spread the cheese over the chicken.
8. Top with the beans, corn, and onion.
9. Return the baking sheet to the oven and broil for 1 minute, or until the cheese melts. Remove from the oven.
10. Drizzle the sour cream mixture and squeeze the lime wedge over the top of the fries.

Baked Chicken Meatballs – Habanero & Green Chili

Prep Time: 10 minutes | Cook Time: 25 minutes | Serves 15 meatballs

- 1 pound ground chicken
- 1 poblano pepper
- 1 habanero pepper
- 1 jalapeno pepper
- 1/2 cup cilantro
- 1 tbsp vinegar
- 1 tbsp olive oil
- salt to taste

1. Preheat broiler to 400 degrees Fahrenheit.
2. In an enormous blending bowl, join chicken, minced peppers, cilantro, salt and vinegar with your hands. Structure 1-inch meatballs with the blend
3. Coat every meatball with olive oil, at that point place on a rimmed heating sheet or meal dish.
4. Heat for 25 minutes.

Chicken Skewer Sandwiches

Prep Time: 20 minutes, plus overnight to marinate | Cook Time: 20 minutes | Serves 4

- ⅔ cup olive oil, plus extra for drizzling
- ⅓ cup red wine vinegar
- 2 lemons, juiced, and one zested
- 4 garlic cloves, chopped
- 1 tablespoon fresh thyme leaves
- 1 tablespoon fresh oregano leaves
- 1 tablespoon fresh basil leaves, rolled and chiffonaded (see Summery Corn and Watermelon Salad, here)
- 1 teaspoon red pepper flakes, or to taste
- 1 bay leaf
- 1 teaspoon cane sugar
- 1 teaspoon kosher salt
- 1 teaspoon freshly ground black pepper
- 1 pound boneless chicken thighs, cut into 1½-inch cubes
- 1 baguette, cut into 4 sections, each split open lengthwise
- 1 tablespoon coarsely chopped fresh mint or parsley, or a mix, for garnish

1. In a large bowl, stir together the olive oil, vinegar, lemon juice and zest, garlic, thyme, oregano, basil, red pepper flakes, bay leaf, sugar, salt, and pepper. Add the cubed chicken and refrigerate, covered tightly or in a large, resealable bag, overnight to marinate.
2. Thread the chicken onto skewers, folding the meat on itself to skewer if it is uneven. Heat a grill pan over high heat until hot. Grill the chicken for 3 to 5 minutes per side, until cooked through and charred in spots.
3. Transfer the grilled skewers to a large plate while you grill the bread. Drizzle olive oil onto the bread and grill for 3 to 5 minutes apiece, rotating as needed, until blackened in spots.
4. These skewers are delicious laid on top of the grilled bread with a scatter of chopped fresh herbs—like parsley or mint—to garnish

Chicken Taquitos

Prep Time: 15 minutes | Cook Time: 13 minutes | Serves 2

- ⅔ cup shredded cooked chicken
- ¼ cup shredded Mexican-style blend cheese or sharp Cheddar cheese
- ¼ cup salsa
- 4 (4½-inch) corn tortillas
- Nonstick cooking spray

1. Preheat the oven to 400° F.
2. Place a wire rack on top of a baking sheet.
3. In a medium bowl, stir together the chicken, cheese, and salsa to combine. Set aside.
4. Fold 4 pieces of paper towel on top of each other and run the stack under water. Gently squeeze the wet towels to remove excess water. Open the damp paper towels and place the corn tortillas between the sheets. Wrap the towels around the tortillas and place them on a microwave-safe plate.
5. Microwave the corn tortillas on high power for 25 seconds. Have your helper remove the tortillas from the microwave, as they will be hot. Unwrap and remove one tortilla, keeping the others covered. Place the tortilla on a clean work surface.
6. Place one-fourth of the chicken mixture into the middle of the tortilla. Wrap the bottom of the tortilla around the mixture, gently pulling it toward you, then roll it up the rest of the way. Place the taquito, seam-side down, onto the wire rack. Spray the taquito with cooking spray. Repeat with the remaining 3 tortillas and filling.
7. Transfer the baking sheet with the rack to the preheated oven and bake for 10 to 12 minutes, until the taquitos are crispy and lightly browned.

Chicken Gyros

Prep Time: 20 minutes plus 1 hour to marinate | Cook Time: 12 minutes | Serves 4 to 6

- For the chicken and the marinade
- 1½ pounds chicken breast tenders
- ¼ cup olive oil
- 2 tablespoons freshly squeezed lemon juice
- 1 teaspoon dried oregano
- 1 teaspoon salt
- For the pitas
- 4 to 6 whole-grain pitas
- ½ to ¾ cup store-bought tzatziki (found in the refrigerated section at your grocery store)
- Red onion slices, for topping (optional)
- Tomato slices, for topping (optional)
- Crumbled feta cheese, for topping (optional)

1. Put the chicken in a large resealable bag. Set it aside.
2. In a small bowl, whisk the oil, lemon juice, oregano, and salt to combine. Pour the marinade over the chicken and seal the bag. Turn the bag to coat the chicken. Refrigerate the chicken in the marinade for at least 1 hour.
3. About 5 minutes before you are ready to cook, position a rack in the oven close to the broiler (ask for help if you need it), and turn the broiler to high.
4. Using tongs, transfer the marinated chicken to an oven-safe grill pan or broiler pan. Discard the marinade. Broil the chicken for 5 minutes. Flip the chicken over and broil for 5 to 7 minutes more, or until the internal temperature reaches 165°F.
5. Wet the paper towel and squeeze out any excess water. Wrap the pitas in the damp paper towel and warm them in the microwave on high power for 25 to 40 seconds before serving. Be careful when removing the pitas from the microwave (use oven mitts); they will be hot.
6. Fill a warm pita with a piece of chicken and some tzatziki. Top with red onion, tomatoes, and feta cheese (if using).

Easy Chicken Tortilla Soup

Prep Time: 15 minutes | Cook Time: 25 minutes | Serves 4

- 8 cups low-sodium chicken broth
- 2 to 3 cups shredded cooked chicken, or 2 (10-ounce) cans chicken, drained
- 1 or 2 (15-ounce) cans black beans, rinsed and drained
- 1 or 2 (15-ounce) cans corn, rinsed and drained, or 1 to 2 cups frozen corn kernels
- 1 (10-ounce) can diced tomatoes and green chilies (I like Ro-Tel)
- 1 (10-ounce) can mild red enchilada sauce
- ½ to 1 cup tortilla chips, crushed
- Cilantro, for topping (optional)
- Sour cream or plain Greek yogurt, for topping (optional)
- Shredded cheese of choice, for topping (optional)
- Sliced scallions, for topping (optional)

1. In a stockpot over medium heat, stir together the chicken broth, chicken, black beans, corn, tomatoes and green chilies, and enchilada sauce.
2. Bring the soup to a boil. Reduce the heat to low and simmer the soup for about 15 minutes.
3. Serve the soup topped with crushed tortilla chips and any additional toppings, as desired.

Chicken Taco Cups

Prep Time: 30 minutes | Cook Time: 40 minutes | Serves 4

- Cooking spray
- 4 large flour tortillas
- 3 tablespoons all-purpose flour
- ½ teaspoon ground cumin
- ½ teaspoon chili powder
- Kosher salt and freshly ground pepper
- 1 pound skinless, boneless chicken breasts, chopped
- 2 tablespoons extra-virgin olive oil
- ½ small onion, finely chopped
- 2 stalks celery, finely chopped
- 2 carrots, finely chopped
- 1 red bell pepper, finely chopped
- 1 14.5-ounce can diced fire-roasted tomatoes
- 1 cup low-sodium chicken broth
- ¼ cup chopped fresh cilantro
- 1 cup shredded monterey jack or pepper jack cheese

1. Preheat the oven to 350°. Coat 4 cups of a muffin pan with cooking spray. Fold each tortilla in half, then form into a cone, overlapping the sides. Fold up the point of each cone slightly, then press the tortillas into the prepared muffin pan to form a cup shape. Coat the tortillas with cooking spray. Bake until golden and crisp, about 15 minutes.
2. Meanwhile, combine the flour, cumin, chili powder, ½ teaspoon salt and a few grinds of pepper in a large bowl. Add the chicken and toss to coat.
3. Heat the olive oil in a large nonstick skillet over medium-high heat. Add the chicken in a single layer and cook, stirring occasionally with a wooden spoon, until lightly browned, about 2 minutes. Add the onion, celery, carrots and bell pepper and cook until the vegetables begin softening, about 2 minutes. Add the tomatoes and chicken broth to the skillet and bring to a simmer. Cook until the vegetables are tender and the sauce thickens slightly, about 5 minutes. Stir in the cilantro and season with salt and pepper.
4. Spoon the chicken mixture into the tortilla cups. Top with the cheese.

Baked Pesto Chicken

Prep Time: 5 minutes | Cook Time: 35 minutes | Serves 4

- 4 chicken breasts about 1.5 lb.
- 3 tbsp basil pesto
- 8 oz mozzarella
- 1/2 tsp salt
- 1/4 tsp black pepper

1. Preheat broiler to 350.
2. Shower heating dish with cooking splash. Spot fowl in the base in a solitary layer and sprinkle with the salt and pepper.
3. Spread the pesto on the bird. Put the mozzarella on top.
4. Heat for 35-45 minutes until the cheddar is excellent and bubbly.
5. Serve.

Keto Crispy Rosemary Chicken Drumsticks

Prep Time: 10 minutes | Cook Time: 40 minutes | Serves 4

- 12 chicken drumsticks
- 4 tbsp of olive oil
- 4 tbsp rosemary leaves
- 2 tsp salt

1. Preheat broiler to 450 F.
2. Focus on salt on every chicken drumstick the blend and spot on a lubed heating plate.
3. Ensure the drumsticks are not contacting each other on the plate. Shower the olive oil or avocado oil over the chicken drumsticks.
4. Prepare for 40 minutes until the skin is firm.

Hawaiian Chicken Kebabs

Prep Time: 25 minutes | Cook Time: 30 minutes | Serves 4

- 1 tablespoon vegetable oil, plus more for brushing
- ¾ cup ketchup
- 3 tablespoons soy sauce or teriyaki sauce
- 3 tablespoons apple cider vinegar
- 1½ tablespoons honey
- 1¼ pounds skinless, boneless chicken breasts, cut into 1¼-inch pieces
- 1 8-ounce can water chestnuts, drained and rinsed (optional)
- 4 cups chopped pineapple
- 1 small red or orange bell pepper, cut into chunks
- Kosher salt and freshly ground pepper
- 4 small Hawaiian sweet rolls

1. Preheat the broiler. Line a baking sheet with foil and brush lightly with vegetable oil.
2. Meanwhile, combine the ketchup, soy sauce, vinegar and honey in a medium bowl and whisk to combine. Spoon half of the sauce into a separate bowl and set aside for dipping.
3. Combine the chicken, water chestnuts, pineapple, bell pepper and 1 tablespoon vegetable oil in a large bowl; sprinkle with ½ teaspoon salt and a few grinds of pepper and toss. Thread the chicken and vegetables onto 8 skewers, alternating the ingredients. Arrange the kebabs on the oiled baking sheet.
4. Brush the kebabs with some of the sauce and broil until the chicken and vegetables start browning, about 4 minutes. Flip the kebabs, brush with more sauce and continue broiling until the chicken is golden and cooked through, about 3 more minutes. Serve with the reserved sauce and rolls.

Buffalo Chicken English Muffin

Prep Time: 10 minutes | Cook Time: 40 minutes | Serves 1

- 1 tablespoon mayonnaise
- 1 tablespoon sour cream
- 1 tablespoon Buffalo hot sauce
- ½ cup shredded rotisserie chicken (skin removed)
- Kosher salt
- 1 English muffin, split
- Unsalted butter, at room temperature, for spreading
- Finely chopped celery and carrots, for topping

1. Mix together the mayonnaise, sour cream and hot sauce in a small bowl. Stir in the chicken and season with salt.
2. Toast the English muffin in a toaster. Spread butter on the cut sides of the English muffin and top with the chicken salad and some celery and carrots.

Chicken Lime Soup

Prep Time: 20 minutes | Cook Time: 30 minutes | Serves 4-6

- Safflower oil, for frying
- 3 corn tortillas, cut into ¼-inch strips
- Flake salt, such as Maldon
- 1 white onion, chopped
- 4 bone-in, skinless chicken thighs
- 3 Roma tomatoes, cored
- 1 serrano or jalapeño chili, cored, seeded, and chopped
- ½ teaspoon dried thyme
- 2 garlic cloves, finely grated
- 3 cups chicken stock
- Juice of 3 limes, plus 2 cut into wedges for serving
- 1½ cups frozen peas, blanched
- 2 avocados, sliced or cubed, for garnish
- Fresh cilantro leaves, for garnish
- Freshly ground black pepper

1. Into a large cast-iron skillet, pour enough oil so that it comes up a quarter inch. Heat the oil, and when very hot, fry the tortilla strips in small batches until golden and crisp, 30 seconds to 1 minute per batch. Tortilla strips should sizzle immediately upon contact with the oil, but not burn. If the oil is smoking, lower the heat.
2. Use a slotted spoon or tongs to transfer the fried tortillas to a paper towel-lined wire cooling rack to soak up excess oil. Sprinkle with a pinch of salt. Repeat until all the tortilla strips have been fried. Set the tortilla strips aside and reserve the oil.
3. In a large saucepan over medium heat, use 1 tablespoon of the frying oil to sauté the onion until translucent, about 5 minutes. Add another tablespoon of the oil, and brown the chicken thighs, turning to brown all sides.
4. Add the tomatoes, jalapeño, thyme, garlic, and stock, and bring the mixture to a boil. Reduce the heat to simmer and cook for 20 minutes, or until the chicken is cooked through, breaking up the tomatoes with the edge of a wooden spoon halfway through simmering.
5. Remove the saucepan from the heat. Use tongs to transfer the chicken from the soup into a large bowl. When cool enough to handle, discard the bones and shred the meat, either with your fingers or using two forks. Return the shredded chicken to the soup, and add the lime juice and peas. Stir thoroughly to combine, taste, and adjust the seasoning as needed.
6. Ladle the soup into bowls, and top with the avocado, cilantro leaves, and fried tortillas. Squeeze the lime wedges over the soup and eat immediately. Allow any leftover soup to come to room temperature, and store refrigerated in sealed containers for up to 3 days. Fried tortilla strips will keep at room temperature, stored between layers of parchment and sealed, for 2 days. Reheat tortillas in the toaster oven or a sauté pan.

Chicken Meatballs in Chickpea Sauce
Prep Time: 10 minutes | Cook Time: 25 minutes | Serves 6

- 1 ¾ oz. milk
- 1 chicken breast fillet
- 2 slices white bread, crust removed
- 1 onion
- 2 cloves garlic
- 1 tablespoon ground black pepper
- Salt, to taste
- 1 lb. minced meat
- 2 tablespoons minced parsley
- 1 egg yolk
- 1 knob butter
- 2 tablespoons tomato puree
- 1 tablespoon Pondicherry red pepper
- 1 teaspoon ras el hanout spice
- 1 handful tinned chickpeas or white beans, drained
- Flaked almonds, to taste
- Minced fresh coriander (optional)

1. Add some olive oil in a casserole dish, sauté the coarsely chopped chicken fillet and onions, and the bread dipped in the milk. Season with salt and black pepper and cook for 5 minutes. Add 4 oz. water and simmer over 275 degrees F.
2. Crush the garlic, black pepper, salt, Ras el hanout and the Pondicherry pepper. Then, in another large bowl, mix the egg yolk, minced meat, butter, bread, 1 tablespoon of parsley, and half of the crushed garlic mix. Shape the mixture into meatballs.
3. Place the meatballs into a casserole, add the tomato paste, chickpeas, the remaining garlic mixture, and 2 oz. of water. Cook until the mixture thickens and sprinkle the remaining parsley. Serve with a sprinkle of silvered almonds and minced coriander.

Roasted Chicken with Onions And Lemons
Prep Time: 10 minutes | Cook Time: 55 minutes | Serves 4

- 1 (3-to 4-pound) whole chicken
- Sea salt
- Freshly ground black pepper
- 1 tablespoon olive oil, plus more for drizzling
- 4 onions, cut into wedges
- 5 lemons, halved
- 1 head garlic, top third cut off
- 5 fresh thyme sprigs

1. Preheat the oven to 425°F.
2. Season the entire chicken well with salt and pepper. Turn it over to season the backside as well as underneath the wings and inside the cavity.
3. Heat a large cast-iron skillet over medium-high heat, add the olive oil, and cook the chicken, breast-side down, until golden brown. Use tongs and a slotted spoon to gently turn the chicken, being careful not to tear the skin. Brown on all sides, 10 to 15 minutes total, and transfer to a plate.
4. In the same skillet, layer the onions in the center, so they'll be underneath the chicken as you roast it. They will soak up the fat and juices, which will make them tender and super flavorful. Add the lemon halves, cut-side down, and the garlic and thyme. Drizzle everything with olive oil.
5. Place the chicken back in the skillet, atop the onion pile. Roast until a meat thermometer inserted into the thickest part of the thigh registers 165°F, 35 to 40 minutes. Another way to see if the chicken is ready is to cut into the thigh meat at the joint. If the juices run clear, it's ready.
6. Before cutting into the chicken, let it rest for 10 to 15 minutes, allowing the internal juices to reabsorb. The roasted chicken is great served alongside the tender caramelized veggies. Spoon the pan juices over all and enjoy!

Creamy Chicken Tortellini Soup

Prep Time: 10 minutes | Cook Time: 35 minutes | Serves 6

- 1 onion
- 4 carrots
- 2 celery stalks
- 4 garlic cloves
- 1 tablespoon canola oil
- 2 teaspoons dried thyme
- 2 large boneless, skinless chicken breasts
- 9 cups chicken broth
- 1 (9-ounce) package tortellini
- 1/3 cup heavy cream
- ½ cup packed baby spinach
- 1 teaspoon table salt
- ½ teaspoon ground black pepper

1. To finely dice the onion, start by cutting the onion in half from root to tip. Peel off the papery outside layer and a layer of onion underneath that. For each onion half, cut off the tip of the onion, but leave the root end intact. Cut each onion half in half again, from root to tip. Place an onion quarter, flat-side down, on a cutting board. Make several vertical cuts from end to end, being careful not to cut through the root end. Flip the onion quarter onto the other flat side and repeat the vertical cuts, again being careful not to cut through the root end. Then cut the onion crosswise into small, even dice—the pieces should just fall off the knife ready to go. Repeat for each onion quarter.
2. Peel the carrots and cut into ¼-inch pieces.
3. Trim the tops and bottoms off the celery. Cut into ¼-inch pieces.
4. Press each garlic clove so it gets a little squished, then peel off the papery layer and cut off the root ends (the nubby side). Moving the knife blade in a rocking motion, run the knife over the squished cloves repeatedly until the garlic is cut into very fine pieces (minced).
5. In a 4-quart stockpot, heat the canola oil over medium-high heat until it shimmers.
6. Add the onion, carrots, celery, and dried thyme. Cook for 5 minutes, or until softened.
7. Add the garlic and cook for 30 seconds.
8. Add the chicken breasts and chicken broth. Bring to a simmer. Cook for 15 minutes, or until a meat thermometer inserted into the thickest part of the chicken reads 165°F.
9. Using tongs, transfer the chicken to a plate and let cool slightly.
10. Add the tortellini to the pot and stir so it doesn't stick. Cook according to the package directions, usually about 10 minutes, until tender.
11. Meanwhile, using 2 forks, shred the chicken until it reaches your desired size for a bite.
12. Once the tortellini have finished cooking, turn off the heat and return the chicken to the pot.
13. Stir in the heavy cream and add the spinach. Season with the salt and pepper.

Curried Chicken Pockets

Prep Time: 25 minutes | Cook Time: 50 minutes | Serves 4

- 1 tablespoon vegetable oil, plus more for brushing
- 1 shallot, finely chopped
- ¾ teaspoon curry powder
- ½ teaspoon grated peeled fresh ginger
- 1 clove garlic, grated
- 1 cup shredded rotisserie chicken (skin removed)
- ¼ cup frozen peas, thawed
- ¼ cup plain low-fat yogurt
- 2 tablespoons chopped fresh cilantro
- 1 teaspoon fresh lime juice
- Kosher salt
- All-purpose flour, for dusting
- 1 11-ounce tube refrigerated French bread dough
- 1 large egg

1. Heat the vegetable oil in a medium skillet over medium heat. Add the shallot, curry powder, ginger and garlic and cook, stirring with a wooden spoon, until the shallot is slightly softened, about 2 minutes. Stir in the chicken. Remove the skillet from the heat.
2. Stir the peas, yogurt, cilantro and lime juice into the chicken mixture. Season with salt. Let the chicken mixture cool completely.
3. Preheat the oven to 425°. Lightly brush a baking sheet with vegetable oil. Lightly dust your work surface with flour. Cut the French bread dough into 4 equal pieces. Using a rolling pin, roll out each piece of dough on the floured surface into a 6-by-8-inch rectangle.
4. Divide the chicken mixture among the dough rectangles, piling it in the center. Fold the 2 shorter sides of the dough over the filling, stretching the dough to cover. Fold in the 2 long sides to enclose. Pinch the seams with your fingers to seal.
5. Move the pockets seam-side down to the oiled baking sheet. Beat the egg and 1 tablespoon water with a fork in a small bowl. Brush the pockets with the egg wash. Bake until golden brown, about 15 minutes. Remove from the oven using oven mitts and let cool slightly.

Cuban Breaded Steak

Prep Time: 15 minutes | Cook Time: 10 minutes | Serves 3

- ¼ cup of olive oil
- ¼ cup of sour orange juice
- 2 tablespoons of n vinegar
- 1 garlic clove minced
- 1 teaspoon of adobo seasoning
- ¼ teaspoon of dried oregano
- 1½ pounds of thinly sliced sirloin steak
- 1 cup of all-purpose flour
- 2 egg whites beaten
- 1 cup of salted soda crackers
- 2 tablespoons of garlic powder
- ½ teaspoon of salt
- Canola oil, for frying

1. Mix the oregano, adobo, garlic, vinegar, orange juice, and olive oil in a shallow bowl. Place the steak in the marinade and mix well. Cover and refrigerate the steak for 4 hours.
2. Blend the garlic powder, salt, and crackers in a food processor. Spread this mixture on a plate. Coat the steaks with flour, dip in the egg whites, and then coat with the breadcrumbs. Set a greased with oil in a skillet over medium heat.
3. Sear the steak for 5 minutes per side. Serve warm.

Pork Tocino

Prep Time: 5 minutes | Cook Time: 15 minutes | Serves 4

- 2 lbs. pork butt, sliced
- 1 cup sugar
- 1 tablespoon salt
- 1 tablespoon garlic powder
- ¼ teaspoon black pepper
- 2 drops red food coloring
- 1 cup water
- 2 tablespoons canola oil

1. Mix the pork with red food color, black pepper, garlic, salt, and sugar in a suitable bowl. Rub the meat with this mixture. Cover and refrigerate this meat overnight. Set a suitable pan over medium heat, add pork, along with marinade, and enough water to cover the pork.
2. Cook this mixture to a boil, reduce its heat and, cover to cook on a simmer until the meat is caramelized. Continue adding more water, if needed. Serve warm.

Fried Meat Patties

Prep Time: 10 minutes | Cook Time: 20 minutes | Serves 6

- 10 oz. beef, minced
- 10 oz. pork, minced
- ½ cup cold water
- 1 egg, beaten
- 1 large onion, chopped
- 5 garlic cloves, chopped
- 1 bunch parsley, chopped
- 2 tablespoon flour
- ½ teaspoon marjoram
- ½ teaspoon ground caraway
- 2 teaspoon lemon juice
- 8 oz. fine breadcrumbs
- 8 tablespoon vegetable oil (for frying)
- Salt, to taste
- Black pepper, to taste
- Chive chopped

1. Mix the minced meats with the water, egg, breadcrumbs, lemon juice, caraway, marjoram, flour, parsley, and garlic in a bowl. Stir in the black pepper and the salt and then knead the dough for 10 minutes.
2. Make 2-inch round balls from this mixture. Flatten the meatballs slightly. Set a skillet with cooking oil over medium heat.
3. Sear the patties for 5 minutes per side. Serve warm.

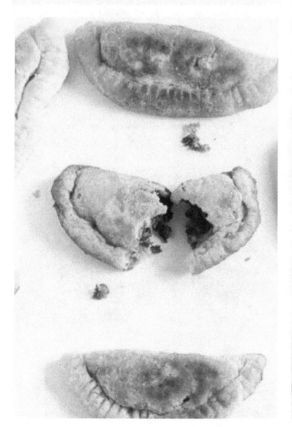

Grilled Pork Skewers with Pomegranate

Prep Time: 10 minutes | Cook Time: 12 minutes | Serves 4

- 2 lbs. boneless pork shoulder, cut into chunks
- 2 medium red onions, grated
- 2 ½ cups red wine vinegar
- 2 teaspoon salt
- 1 teaspoon black pepper
- ½ cup pomegranate arils
- Spicy Bell Pepper Jam
- Sour Plum Sauce

1. Mix the pork with black pepper, salt, red wine vinegar, and red onion in a bowl. Next, cover and refrigerate for 4 hours.
2. Thread the pork on the metal skewers and cover to marinate for 30 minutes. Set a grill on high heat and grease its grilling grates with cooking oil. Grill the skewers for 12 minutes. Toss the pomegranate arils, onion slices, black pepper and salt.
3. Serve the skewers with the onion salsa, pepper jam and plum sauce. Enjoy.

Ham and Cheese Wafflewiches with Kale Chips

Prep Time: 30 minutes | Cook Time: 30 minutes | Serves 4

- For the kale chips
- 1 bunch Tuscan kale (about 1 pound)
- 1 tablespoon extra-virgin olive oil
- Kosher salt
- For the sandwiches
- 1 Granny Smith apple, peeled and grated on the large holes of a box grater
- ⅓ cup honey mustard
- 8 frozen waffles
- ½ pound sliced deli ham
- ¼ pound sliced cheddar cheese
- 2 tablespoons unsalted butter, plus more if needed

1. Make the kale chips: Preheat the oven to 275°. Carefully cut off the tough stems of the kale with a chef's knife; discard. Chop the kale leaves into 1½-inch pieces. Toss the kale on a baking sheet with the olive oil and ½ teaspoon salt and spread in a single layer.
2. Bake the kale for 10 minutes, then remove the baking sheet from the oven with oven mitts and flip the kale leaves with tongs or a spatula. Put back in the oven and continue to bake until the kale leaves are crisp, about 10 more minutes.
3. Meanwhile, make the sandwiches: Stir together the grated apple with the honey mustard in a medium bowl until combined. Spoon the apple mixture on 4 waffles and spread evenly. Top with the ham, cheese and remaining waffles to make 4 sandwiches.
4. Melt the butter in a large nonstick skillet over medium heat. Carefully add the sandwiches and cook, flipping once with a spatula, until golden, about 3 minutes per side. Add more butter to the skillet when you flip the sandwich, if needed. Serve with the kale chips.

Minty Lamb Burgers

Prep Time: 10 minutes | Cook Time: 12-15 minutes | Serves 4

- 1½ pounds ground lamb
- 1 garlic clove, finely grated
- 3 tablespoons finely chopped fresh mint
- 3 tablespoons finely chopped fresh parsley
- ½ teaspoon cumin seeds, toasted and ground in a mortar and pestle (see No-Nonsense Guacamole, here)
- Kosher salt
- Freshly ground black pepper
- Olive oil, for brushing
- Ciabatta rolls, for serving
- Easy Tzatziki (here), for serving
- Romaine lettuce leaves, for serving

1. In a medium bowl, gently mix together the lamb with the garlic, mint, parsley, cumin, and a pinch each of salt and pepper. Divide the meat into 4 patties of equal size and thickness—about 1/2 inch thick—and transfer to a plate. Press a small dimple in the center of each patty with two fingers to offset how it shrinks as it cooks. Lightly brush the burgers with olive oil, and season again with salt and pepper.
2. Heat the grill pan over high heat. When it's hot, brush the grate lightly with olive oil. Grill the patties over medium heat for 7 to 8 minutes for medium-rare or 8 to 10 minutes for medium, turning halfway through. Transfer them to a plate.
3. Slice the ciabatta in half horizontally, brush lightly with olive oil, and place cut-side down on the grill pan. Grill long enough to allow the bread to char in spots, 3 to 5 minutes.
4. Put the bread on plates and top with the burgers. Garnish with the Easy Tzatziki, romaine, and any delicious additions.

Spaghetti with Cheeseburger Meatballs

Prep Time: 45 minutes | Cook Time: 50 minutes | Serves 6

- Kosher salt
- 12 ounces spaghetti
- 3 stale hamburger buns
- 2 tablespoons extra-virgin olive oil
- ½ cup whole milk
- 1 pound ground beef
- ½ cup finely chopped onion
- ¼ cup finely chopped dill pickle slices, plus pickle slices for serving
- ¼ cup ketchup
- 1 tablespoon yellow mustard
- 1 tablespoon Worcestershire sauce
- Freshly ground pepper
- 1½ ounces sharp white cheddar cheese, cut into 24 small cubes, plus grated cheese for topping
- 4 cloves garlic, sliced
- 2 tablespoons tomato paste
- Thinly sliced romaine lettuce and chopped tomato, for topping

1. Preheat the oven to 350°. Fill a large pot with water and season with salt. Bring to a boil over high heat. Add the spaghetti and cook as the label directs for al dente. Carefully remove 1 cup of the pasta cooking water with a liquid measuring cup; set aside. Carefully drain the spaghetti in a colander set in the sink.

2. Meanwhile, put 2 hamburger buns in a food processor and pulse into coarse crumbs. Heat 1 tablespoon olive oil in a large nonstick skillet over medium heat. Add the breadcrumbs and cook, stirring, until toasted, about 3 minutes, then spoon into a bowl. Bunch up a paper towel and hold it with tongs to wipe out the skillet.

3. Tear up the remaining hamburger bun; put in a large bowl along with the milk and let soak 5 minutes. Drain, squeezing the excess milk from the bread. Return the soaked bread to the empty bowl and add half of the toasted breadcrumbs, the ground beef, onion, chopped pickles, 2 tablespoons ketchup, the mustard, Worcestershire sauce, ½ teaspoon salt and a few grinds of pepper. Mix with your hands until combined. Divide the meat mixture into 24 pieces. Press a cheese cube into the center of each and shape into meatballs around the cheese.

4. Heat the remaining 1 tablespoon olive oil in the same skillet over medium heat. Add the meatballs and cook, turning with the tongs, until browned, about 4 minutes. Arrange the meatballs on a rimmed baking sheet; place in the oven and bake until just cooked through, about 5 minutes. Reserve the skillet.

5. Add the garlic to the skillet; cook over medium heat until golden, about 30 seconds. Add the tomato paste and the remaining 2 tablespoons ketchup; cook 1 minute, then stir in the reserved pasta cooking water until smooth. Simmer until slightly thickened, about 3 minutes.

6. Add the spaghetti to the skillet and toss to coat with the tongs. Use the tongs to serve the spaghetti and top with the remaining toasted breadcrumbs, the meatballs, grated cheddar, lettuce and tomato. Serve with pickle slices.

Chimichurri Steak

Prep Time: 15 minutes, plus 20 minutes to rest | Cook Time: 10 minutes, plus 10 minutes to rest | Serves 4

- 4 pieces strip steak, rib eye steak, or fillet steaks
- ½ teaspoon kosher salt, plus more for seasoning the steak
- ¼ teaspoon freshly ground black pepper, plus more for seasoning the steak
- 5 garlic cloves, chopped
- 2 tablespoons fresh oregano leaves
- 1 teaspoon red pepper flakes
- ¼ cup chopped fresh parsley
- ¼ cup chopped fresh cilantro
- 3 tablespoons red wine vinegar
- ½ cup grapeseed or olive oil, plus more if needed

1. Pat the steaks dry with a paper towel. Season well with kosher salt and pepper, and set aside to rest at room temperature for 20 to 30 minutes.

2. In a food processor or high-powered blender, combine the garlic, oregano, red pepper flakes, parsley, cilantro, and vinegar. Pulse until the garlic and greens are finely chopped and the sauce is blended. Pour into a small bowl and set aside.

3. In a large, heavy skillet or cast-iron pan over medium-high heat, heat the oil. Swirl the oil around to coat the pan. Once the oil begins to shimmer and the first wisp of smoke appears, add the steaks, leaving room in between. Cook for 3 to 5 minutes on one side (see Helpful Hint), then use tongs to turn the steaks over and cook to desired doneness or until a meat thermometer inserted in the thickest part of the steak reads 145°F, for medium (see chart here). Add more oil if the pan looks dry.

4. Remove the steaks from the pan and allow them to rest for 5 to 10 minutes without touching them. Transfer the steaks to a serving plate, spoon a line of chimichurri sauce down the middle of each, and serve.

Meatloaf Rolls

Prep Time: 5 minutes | Cook Time: 25 minutes | Serves 6

- 1 pound ground beef
- 1 pound ground pork
- 2 eggs
- 1 onion, chopped
- 3 garlic cloves, crushed
- 2 tablespoon dried marjoram
- Salt and ground pepper, to taste
- ¾ cups bread crumbs
- 1 package sliced bacon

1. At 350 degrees F, preheat your oven.
2. Mix the beef with the pork, eggs, onion, garlic, marjoram, black pepper, salt, and breadcrumbs in a bowl. Divide the meat mixture into 3 portions and shape them into meatloaves. Wrap the meatloaves with the bacon slices and seal them with a twine.
3. Place the meatloaves in a baking sheet and bake for 25 minutes or more until golden brown. Slice and serve.

Chinese Meatball Sliders with Pineapple Salad

Prep Time: 30 minutes | Cook Time: 30 minutes | Serves 4

- 2 tablespoons hoisin sauce
- 2 tablespoons plus 1 teaspoon rice vinegar (not seasoned)
- 12 ounces ground pork
- 2 tablespoons panko
- 1 scallion (white and light green parts only), sliced
- 1 teaspoon grated peeled ginger
- Kosher salt and freshly ground pepper
- ¼ small head green cabbage, chopped
- 2 small carrots, chopped
- ½ cup chopped pineapple
- 1 tablespoon mayonnaise, plus more for the buns
- 12 mini potato slider buns
- Shredded romaine lettuce, for topping

1. Position a rack in the upper third of the oven and preheat to 425°. Coat a rimmed baking sheet with cooking spray. Combine 1 tablespoon hoisin sauce and 1 teaspoon rice vinegar in a small bowl; set aside.
2. Combine the pork, panko, the remaining 1 tablespoon hoisin sauce, the scallion, ginger, ½ teaspoon salt and a few grinds of pepper in a medium bowl. Mix with your hands until combined, then roll the mixture into twelve 1½-inch meatballs; put on the prepared baking sheet. Bake until browned, 5 to 6 minutes, then carefully remove from the oven with oven mitts and turn the meatballs with tongs. Return to the oven and bake until browned and cooked through, 5 to 6 more minutes. Remove from the oven and brush with the reserved hoisin sauce mixture.
3. Meanwhile, combine the cabbage, carrots, pineapple, the remaining 2 tablespoons rice vinegar, the mayonnaise and ½ teaspoon salt in a food processor and pulse until the vegetables and pineapple are roughly chopped.
4. Spread mayonnaise on the bottom half of each bun, then fill with some shredded lettuce and a meatball. Serve with the pineapple salad.

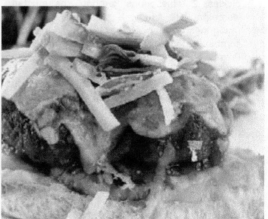

Pulled Pork Sliders

Prep Time: 15 minutes plus 1 hour to rest | Cook Time: 3 hours 40 minutes | Serves 8

- 2 teaspoons whole coriander seeds
- 2 teaspoons whole cumin seeds
- 2 tablespoons dark brown sugar
- 1 tablespoon kosher salt
- 1 teaspoon freshly ground black pepper
- 1 tablespoon paprika
- 1½ teaspoons dry mustard powder
- ¼ teaspoon ground cayenne pepper
- 1 (6-to 8-pound) bone-in pork shoulder, preferably skin-on
- ½ cup apple cider vinegar
- 2 tablespoons cane sugar
- Pinch red pepper flakes
- Toasted buns, for serving
- 1 recipe Savory Cabbage Slaw, for serving

1. In a small, dry cast-iron skillet over medium heat, toast the coriander and cumin until fragrant, about 1 to 2 minutes. Use a mortar and pestle to grind the toasted spices into a powder.
2. In a small bowl, mix together the brown sugar, salt, pepper, coriander, cumin, paprika, mustard powder, and cayenne in a small bowl, mixing with your fingers or a fork until well combined.
3. Rub the spice mixture over the entire surface of the pork, caking as much of it onto the meat as you can. If you have time, let the meat rest 1 to 2 hours at room temperature before roasting, or refrigerate overnight, loosely wrapped in plastic and set on a tray.
4. Preheat the oven to 325°F.
5. Place the pork on a foil-lined, rimmed baking sheet, skin-side-up, and roast for 3 to 3½ hours, or until the meat is pull-apart tender.
6. Transfer the pork to a large bowl, and let it rest at least 20 minutes.
7. Use tongs to carefully lift the skin off. Raise the oven temperature to 500°F. Use a fork to scrape any clinging meat into the bowl. Remove the fat from the skin and discard, returning the skin to the baking sheet. Roast the skin for 5 to 10 minutes, until crisp and bubbly. Remove from the oven and set aside.
8. Shred the pork using two forks or your hands. Save bones for stock or discard. Finely chop the skin, and combine it with the meat, removing any visible fat. Season the meat with salt and pepper. Stir together the vinegar, cane sugar, and a pinch of red pepper flakes, and add to the mixture to taste.
9. Serve the pulled pork hot, piled on toasted buns and topped with Savory Cabbage Slaw. Store the pulled pork for up to 4 days refrigerated in a sealed container. It also keeps frozen for up to 1 month.

Savory Beef Ragù

Prep Time: 15 minutes | Cook Time: 1 hour 40 minutes | Serves 4

- 2 strips thick-cut bacon, diced
- 1 onion, chopped
- 2 carrots, scrubbed and chopped
- 2 celery stalks, chopped
- 4 garlic cloves, finely grated
- 1 fennel bulb, sliced
- 3 anchovy filets
- 1 pound ground beef
- ½ cup dry red wine
- 2 fresh thyme sprigs, leaves stripped from stems
- 1 bay leaf
- ½ teaspoon red chili flakes
- ⅛ teaspoon freshly grated nutmeg
- ⅛ teaspoon ground cinnamon
- 1 (28-ounce) can whole plum tomatoes
- 1 tablespoon tomato paste
- 1 cup beef stock
- 2 teaspoons balsamic vinegar
- 2 teaspoons Worcestershire sauce
- Kosher salt
- Freshly ground black pepper

1. In a Dutch oven or other heavy-bottomed pot over medium heat, cook the bacon until just crispy, about 7 minutes. Remove the bacon from the fat, and set aside.
2. Sauté the onion in the bacon fat until translucent, stirring occasionally, about 10 minutes. Add the carrots and celery, stir to combine, and cook for another 5 minutes or until lightly browned. Add the garlic, fennel, and anchovies, making a little room at the base of the pot for the anchovies. As they begin to sizzle, break the anchovies up with the edge of a wooden spoon and stir to incorporate.
3. Add the ground beef and bacon to the pot. Sauté until lightly browned, 5 to 7 minutes, stirring and breaking up meat as you did the anchovies. Add the wine, and as it bubbles, scrape the bottom of the pot to free up any browned bits. Reduce the wine by half, stirring occasionally, then add the thyme, bay leaf, chili flakes, nutmeg, cinnamon, tomatoes, tomato paste, beef stock, vinegar, and Worcestershire sauce. Give a good stir to bring the mixture together.
4. Taste, season with salt and pepper as needed, and cover. Turn the heat to low so that it bubbles slowly. After 10 minutes or so, break the softened tomatoes into chunks using the edge of a wooden spoon.
5. Cover again and simmer for another 45 minutes to 1 hour, or until the ingredients have melded and the sauce has thickened. Season with salt and pepper.
6. Serve hot directly from the pot set on a trivet at the table. This dish is fantastic tossed with cooked pasta or alongside crusty bread.

Cuban Mojo Pork

Prep Time: 10 minutes, plus 2 hours to marinate | Cook Time: 25 minutes | Serves 6

- ½ cup grapeseed or olive oil
- ¾ cup freshly squeezed orange juice, plus the zest of 2 oranges, zested, then juiced (¾ cup)
- ¼ cup freshly squeezed lime juice
- Large handful fresh cilantro (about ½ cup)
- 4 tablespoons garlic paste or 4 garlic cloves
- 1 tablespoon fresh oregano leaves
- 12 fresh mint leaves
- Kosher salt
- Freshly ground black pepper
- 3 pounds pork tenderloin (typically 2 pieces in a package, each weighing 1¼ to 1½ pounds)

1. In a food processor or blender, combine the oil, orange juice, lime juice, cilantro, garlic, oregano, and mint, and pulse until the leaves and garlic are minced and the marinade is liquid. Toss in the orange zest, and stir to combine.
2. Season the pork with salt and pepper, place in a shallow baking dish, and pour the marinade over top. Cover and refrigerate for 2 to 24 hours, turning the pork occasionally to coat in the marinade.
3. Make sure the grill is clean and oiled. Preheat the grill to medium-high, and place the pork directly onto the grates. Discard the marinade. Once grill marks appear on the bottom and the meat releases itself, after 3 to 4 minutes, turn the meat a quarter turn. Continue to cook, turning occasionally, for 12 to 14 minutes more. Pork is done when the internal temperature at the thickest part of the tenderloins is 145°F (see Pro Tip). Remove from the grill, tent with foil, and let rest for 5 minutes. Slice and serve.

Steak Tacos

Prep Time: 25 minutes | Cook Time: 10 minutes, plus 10 minutes to rest | Serves 6

- ½ tablespoon salt
- 1 teaspoon chili powder
- 1 teaspoon onion powder
- ½ teaspoon freshly ground black pepper
- 1½ pounds flank steak
- 2 to 3 carrots
- 1 small red cabbage
- Lemon Vinaigrette
- ½ tablespoon grapeseed or olive oil, plus more if needed
- ½ recipe Avocado Dip or guacamole, plus more for serving
- Flour tortillas, for serving
- Chips, for serving

1. In a small bowl, combine the salt, chili powder, onion powder, and pepper, and mix until blended. Rub the seasoning mix onto both sides of the steak, and allow the steak to sit at room temperature for 20 minutes.
2. Using the larger side of a grater, shred the carrots by holding the carrot on an angle for longer shreds (you should have about 1½ cups). Place the shredded carrots in a medium bowl. Quarter a small head of red cabbage, remove the core from one of the quarters. Slice the quarter crosswise into thin strips and place in the bowl with the carrots (you should have about 1 cup). Toss with the Lemon Vinaigrette, and, using your hands, massage the dressing into the shredded vegetables a bit. Set aside and allow the flavors to mingle.
3. In a large skillet or sauté pan over medium-high heat, heat the oil. Once the oil begins to shimmer and a first wisp of smoke comes off of it, carefully place the steak in the pan. Cook the steak until a meat thermometer registers 145°F for medium (see chart here), typically 4 to 5 minutes per side, turning once with tongs. Add additional oil if the pan looks dry, and reduce the heat if the meat is starting to burn.
4. Transfer the steak to a cutting board and allow to rest for 10 minutes. Using a chef's knife or serrated bread knife, slice the steak into thin slices, going against the grain (see Pro Tip).
5. Assemble the tacos by placing the meat, Avocado Dip, and the vegetable slaw onto tortillas. Serve chips alongside with extra Avocado Dip.

Meatloaf Sub

Prep Time: 15 minutes | Cook Time: 1 hour 40 minutes | Serves 4

- 1½ lbs. lean ground beef
- 1/3 cup Italian seasoned breadcrumbs
- ½ small onion, diced
- 1 tsp salt
- ½ cup shredded mozzarella cheese, divided
- 1 Tbsp cracked black pepper
- 1 tsp garlic powder
- ½ cup marinara sauce
- 3 hoagie rolls, split lengthwise

1. Preheat oven to 350°F.
2. In a bowl, combine ½ of the mozzarella, beef, garlic powder, bread crumbs, pepper, onions, and salt.
3. Shape the mix into a large loaf, then place it in a casserole dish.
4. Cook the meat in the oven for 55 minutes then let it cool for 10 minutes.
5. Cut the meat into slices, then layer the pieces of meat on a roll.
6. Top everything with the marinara, then remaining cheese.
7. Cover the sandwich with foil and bake for 20 more minutes.
8. Let the sandwich cool for 20 minutes, then cut each one in half.

Sweet And Sour Ground Beef

Prep Time: 10 minutes | Cook Time: 10 minutes | Serves 6

- 1 lb. ground beef
- 2 tomatoes, diced
- ¼ cup yellow mustard
- 1 Tbsp balsamic vinegar
- 1 Tbsp minced garlic
- 1½ tsp soy sauce
- 1½ tsp honey
- 1½ tsp paprika

1. Cook beef over medium heat in a skillet for about 7 minutes, or until brown.
2. Add remaining ingredients and cook for another three minutes.

Mexican Style Tijuna Ground Beef

Prep Time: 10 minutes | Cook Time: 40 minutes | Serves 4

- 1 lb. ground beef
- 1 cup salsa
- ½ cup water
- 1 green bell pepper, diced
- 1 bunch green onions, diced
- 1 (8 ounces) package wide egg noodles
- ½ cup sour cream
- ½ cup shredded Cheddar cheese
- 1 tomato, diced

1. In a skillet, cook ground beef until browned.
2. Stir in water and salsa, and cook for 10 minutes.
3. Add onions and green pepper into the pan, and cook until the veggies are tender.
4. Add cooked noodles, grated cheese, and sour cream.
5. Cover until the cheese melts, then top with tomatoes.

Spicy Beef and Broccoli Stir-Fry

Prep Time: 20 minutes | Cook Time: 8 minutes | Serves 6

- 3 Tbsp dry sherry
- 3 Tbsp soy sauce
- 4 large garlic cloves, minced
- 1 tsp Asian (dark) sesame oil
- ¼ tsp red pepper flakes
- ½ pound beef tenderloin, trimmed and cut into strips
- 1 tsp cornstarch
- 2 tsp canola oil
- 4 cups broccoli florets
- 2 cups hot, cooked brown rice

1. Stir together sherry, soy sauce, garlic, sesame oil, and pepper flakes in a one- cup measuring cup. Transfer ¼ cup of the mixture to a large zip-close plastic bag;
2. Add beef. Squeeze out air and seal bag; turn over to coat beef. Refrigerate, turning bag, for at least 1 hour or up to 2 hours.
3. Add cornstarch and enough water to soy sauce mixture in the cup to bring the volume to 1/3 cup; stir mixture until smooth.
4. Heat a large skillet over high heat until a drop of water sizzles in the pan; add canola oil and swirl to coat pan. Add beef and stir-fry for 2 minutes. Transfer beef to a plate. Add broccoli to wok; stir-fry 3 minutes, then cover and cook 1 minute. Restir cornstarch mixture; add it to the wok along with the beef. Stir-fry until sauce bubbles and thickens, about 2 minutes. Serve with rice.

Chapter 6
Fish and Seafood

Cod with Tomato and Chorizo Sauce

Prep Time: 15 minutes | Cook Time: 20 minutes | Serves 4

- 1 teaspoon olive oil
- 1 garlic clove, sliced
- 4 chorizo thin slices, cut into matchsticks
- 1 pinch dried chilli flakes
- 14 oz. tin tomatoes, chopped
- 2 thick skinless white fish fillets
- Green beans cooked, to serve

1. In a pan, heat 1 tablespoon olive oil and sauté the garlic and chorizo for a few minutes. Season with salt and pepper after adding the chilies and tomatoes and simmering for 10 minutes until thickened.
2. Meanwhile, brush the fish with a little extra oil, season with salt and pepper, and grill or steam until done, about 4-6 minutes.
3. Serve the fish with a side of green beans and the sauce.

Sesame Drizzled Shrimp Veggie Bowl

Prep Time: 10 minutes | Cook Time: 22 minutes | Serves 4

- 1 pound (454 g) shrimp, cleaned and deveined
- 2 cups cauliflower, cut into florets
- 2 green bell pepper, sliced
- 1 shallot, sliced
- 2 tablespoons sesame oil
- 1 cup tomato paste
- Cooking spray

1. Select the BAKE function and preheat MAXX to 360°F (182°C). Spritz a baking pan with cooking spray.
2. Arrange the shrimp and vegetables in the baking pan. Then, drizzle the sesame oil over the vegetables.
3. Pour the tomato paste over the vegetables. Bake for 10 minutes in the preheated air fryer oven. Stir with a large spoon and bake for a further 12 minutes. Serve warm.

Mock Oyster Stew

Prep Time: 10 minutes | Cook Time: 20 minutes | Serves 2

- 1 cup canned or fresh mushrooms
- 2 cups chicken broth
- ¼ cup milk
- 1 tsp soy sauce
- Black pepper, to taste

1. If using fresh mushrooms, wipe clean with a damp cloth. Slice the mushrooms.
2. Bring the chicken broth and milk to a boil in a medium-sized saucepan.
3. Add the mushrooms.
4. Bring back to a boil, and stir in the soy sauce and black pepper. Taste and adjust the seasoning if desired.

Curried Tuna Melt English Muffin

Prep Time: 10 minutes | Cook Time: 10 minutes | Serves 1

- 2 tablespoons mayonnaise
- ½ teaspoon curry powder
- 1 3-ounce can tuna, drained
- 1 scallion, thinly sliced
- Kosher salt and freshly ground pepper
- 1 English muffin, split
- 2 small slices cheddar cheese
- Sweet potato chips, for topping

1. Preheat the broiler. Mix together the mayonnaise and curry powder in a small bowl. Stir in the tuna and scallion. Season with salt and pepper.
2. Toast the English muffin in a toaster. Spread the tuna mixture on the cut sides of the English muffin. Top each half with a slice of cheese.
3. Place the English muffin halves on a baking sheet, carefully place under the broiler and broil until the cheese is melted, about 3 minutes. Top with sweet potato chips.

Shrimp Spinach Egg Bake

Prep Time: 10 minutes | Cook Time: 14 minutes | Serves 4

- 4 whole eggs
- 1 teaspoon dried basil
- ½ cup shrimp, cooked and chopped
- ½ cup baby spinach
- ½ cup rice, cooked
- ½ cup Monterey Jack cheese, grated
- Salt, to taste
- Cooking spray

1. Spritz a baking pan with cooking spray.
2. Whisk the eggs with basil and salt in a large bowl until bubbly, then mix in the shrimp, spinach, rice, and cheese. Pour the mixture into the baking pan. Select the BAKE function.
3. Set Air Fryer temperature to 360°F (182°C) and set time to 14 minutes. Press Start to begin preheating. Once preheated, place the pan into the oven.
4. Stir the mixture halfway through. When cooking is complete, the eggs should be set and the frittata should be golden brown. Slice to serve.

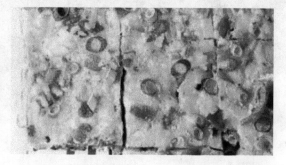

Pan-Roasted Fish

Prep Time: 5 minutes | Cook Time: 10 minutes | Serves 4

- 4 (5-ounce) skin-on fish fillets (such as red snapper, flounder, haddock, or salmon), ½ to 1 inch thick
- Kosher salt
- Freshly ground black pepper
- 4 tablespoons olive oil
- 3 tablespoons butter
- 3 fresh thyme sprigs, leaves stripped from stems, coarsely chopped
- Chopped fresh parsley and lemon wedges (optional), for garnish

1. Pat the fish dry with paper towels and season on both sides with salt and pepper.
2. Place a large cast-iron skillet over high heat. When the skillet is hot, add the oil. Place the fillets skin-side down away from you into the pan, so if any splattering happens, you'll have less risk of being burned. Press down gently with a metal spatula for about 20 seconds around the edges so that the fillets don't curl up.
3. Lower the heat to medium and let sizzle until the fish is caramelized and becoming opaque around the edges, 2 to 3 minutes. Carefully flip the fillets to the second side, and add the butter and thyme to the pan.
4. Tilt the pan slightly to pool the melted butter on one side. Use a spoon to baste the fish with the melted butter. Baste the fillets repeatedly, until they are golden all over and cooked through, 1 minute or so, depending on the thickness of your fish.
5. Serve immediately, with chopped parsley and lemon wedges, if desired.

Garlic Shrimp

Prep Time: 15 minutes | Cook Time: 5 minutes | Serves 4

- 3 tablespoons olive oil
- 8 garlic cloves, chopped
- 2 pounds large shrimp (21 to 25 count), cleaned, shells and tails removed
- Kosher salt
- Freshly ground black pepper
- 1 stick butter, cut into 6 chunks, divided
- ⅓ cup freshly squeezed lemon juice
- ¼ cup capers, and a splash of caper juice
- Ground cayenne pepper
- 2 tablespoons chopped fresh parsley

1. In a large sauté pan over medium-high heat, heat the oil. Add the garlic and sauté for 30 seconds. Add the shrimp and sauté for 1 to 2 minutes. Reduce the heat to medium, and sprinkle with salt and black pepper.
2. Add 3 chunks of butter and the lemon juice, and continue to cook, turning occasionally, until no longer pink and cooked through, about 2 more minutes.
3. Remove from the heat, add the capers and juice,

sprinkle with the cayenne pepper and parsley, and add the remaining 3 chunks of butter. Toss until the butter is melted, and serve immediately.

Fresh Fish Tacos

Prep Time: 15 minutes, plus 50 minutes to marinate | Cook Time: 15 minutes | Serves 4

- ½ red onion, sliced thin
- Pinch black peppercorns
- 1 bay leaf
- ¾ cup white vinegar
- 1 teaspoon cumin seeds, toasted (see the No-Nonsense Guacamole, here)
- ⅓ cup olive oil
- 1½ teaspoons chili powder
- ¼ cup chopped fresh cilantro leaves, plus more for garnish
- ½ to 1 jalapeño pepper, seeded and minced
- Kosher salt
- 1 pound flaky white fish (such as flounder, red snapper, or cod), cut into 4 pieces
- Freshly ground black pepper
- 8 fresh corn or flour tortillas
- 1 recipe of Salsa Fresca (here) and/or Savory Cabbage Slaw (here), for serving
- Sour cream, for serving
- 2 limes, quartered

1. In a small mason jar with a lid, arrange the onion slices, adding a pinch of peppercorns and a bay leaf, and pour in enough white vinegar to cover. Set aside to marinate for at least 30 minutes.
2. Grind the toasted cumin into a coarse powder with a mortar and pestle. In a small bowl, mix the olive oil, chili powder, cumin, chopped cilantro, and jalapeño, and season with salt. Place the fillets on a baking sheet and pour the marinade over, making sure to coat the fillets well on both sides. Marinate for 20 minutes at room temperature.
3. Heat the broiler with the oven rack in the highest position. Season the fish with salt and pepper. Broil until the fillets are browned on top and the flesh is opaque throughout, about 5 minutes. Remove the pan from the oven and flake the fish with a fork. Taste and adjust seasoning as needed, then set aside.
4. Lower the oven temperature to 400°F. Place the tortillas in two stacks of 4, and wrap the bundles in aluminum foil. Heat in the oven for 7 to 10 minutes, until the tortillas are warmed through. Place the tortillas, still wrapped in foil, in a tea towel to keep warm.
5. To assemble the tacos, place a heaping spoonful of Savory Cabbage Slaw on the center of a tortilla. Add the flaked fish and Salsa Fresca, and top with the marinated onions. Serve accompanied by cilantro sprigs, sour cream, and lime wedges.

Miso-Grilled Shrimp Skewers

Prep Time: 20 minutes plus 20 minutes to marinate | Cook Time: 5-7 minutes | Serves 4

- 2 tablespoons freshly squeezed lime juice, with extra wedges for garnish
- 2 tablespoons mirin
- 2 tablespoons yellow miso
- 1 tablespoon sesame oil
- 1 tablespoon fresh ginger, peeled and finely grated
- 1 large garlic clove, finely grated
- 1 pound large shrimp, shelled and deveined

1. In a large bowl, whisk together the lime juice, mirin, miso, sesame oil, ginger, and garlic. Add the shrimp, and toss to coat. Let marinate for 20 minutes.
2. Preheat a grill pan over medium-high heat. Thread the shrimp onto metal skewers, piercing the shrimp at the tail end and at the thickest part of the body to secure. Grill the shrimp over medium-high heat until lightly charred and opaque, turning once, about 5 minutes.
3. These glazed and grilled shrimp are great served in steamed buns with chopped fresh scallions and cilantro, over rice, or alongside crunchy green beans, greens, or Asian Cucumber Salad.

Shrimp Toast

Prep Time: 5 minutes | Cook Time: 25 minutes | Serves 6

- 5 white bread slices, crust removed, and cut into 4 triangles diagonally
- ½ pound raw shrimp, peeled, and deveined
- 2 teaspoons lard
- 4 water chestnuts, chopped
- ½ tomato, chopped
- 2 scallions, chopped
- 1 teaspoon fresh ginger, grated
- 1 teaspoon Chinese rice wine
- 1 large egg, beaten lightly
- 2 teaspoons cornstarch
- Salt and black pepper, or to taste
- 4 cups canola oil

1. Preheat the oven to 225 degrees F. Arrange the bread slices onto a 9x13-inch non-stick baking sheet in a single layer. Bake for 25-30 minutes.
2. Meanwhile, in a food processor with a knife blade, add the shrimp and lard and pulse until chopped. Add the water chestnuts, tomato, scallion, and ginger and pulse until combined. Add the remaining ingredients except the oil and pulse smooth. Spread about 2 teaspoons of the shrimp paste over each toasted bread slice evenly.
3. In a deep skillet, heat the oil to 350 degrees F and deep fry the toasts in 3-4 batches for about 1½ minutes. Flip and cook for about 15 seconds. With a slotted spoon, transfer the toasts onto a paper towel-lined plate to drain. Serve warm.

Fish in Parchment Paper

Prep Time: 1 hour | Cook Time: 20 minutes | Serves 4

- 4 filets mild white fish (such as cod, tilapia, sole, or turbot)
- ½ cup mild extra-virgin olive oil, divided
- 1 teaspoon lemon pepper (optional)
- 1 medium eggplant
- 1 medium zucchini
- 1 medium summer squash
- 1 lemon
- 8 cooked shrimp (optional)
- 2 cups grape tomatoes

1. Place the fish in a zip-top plastic bag with 1 tablespoon of the olive oil and the lemon pepper, if using, to lightly coat the fish. Place the sealed bag in the refrigerator for 1 hour to marinate.
2. Preheat the oven to 350°F.
3. Cut the eggplant, zucchini, squash, and lemon into round slices.
4. Roll out parchment paper on a flat surface. Remove the fish from the refrigerator and place one fillet on the paper. Cut the paper so that there is a 4- to 6-inch margin of paper around each side of the fish. Place 1 to 2 slices of eggplant underneath the fish. On top of the fish, place 1 to 2 slices of lemon. Place 2 of the shrimp, if using, on top of the lemon and fish. Top with 3 to 4 grape tomatoes. Add ¼ of the zucchini and squash all around the sides of the fish so that the vegetables are on their sides leaning against the fish. Sprinkle with the remaining olive oil. Fold the paper around the fish like a present and wrap it with butchers' twine to secure the paper. Repeat for each fillet.
5. Place the wrapped fish filets on the center oven rack, with a baking sheet on the rack below to catch any juices, and bake in the preheated oven for 20 minutes, or until the fish flakes easily with a fork. Thicker filets may require additional cooking time.
6. Place a wrapped fish on each guest's plate and cut the parchment open. Serve in the juices inside the parchment paper.

Roasted Salmon

Prep Time: 15 minutes | Cook Time: 12 minutes | Serves 4

- 4 tablespoons unsalted butter
- Coarse salt and ground pepper, to taste
- 1 (3 pounds) salmon fillet, skin on
- Chopped fresh parsley leaves, for serving

1. At 375 degrees F, preheat your oven.
2. Grease a rimmed baking sheet with butter.
3. Place the salmon in the baking sheet and brush the fish with butter, black pepper and salt.
4. Bake the salmon for 12 minutes in the preheated oven.
5. Garnish with parsley and serve warm.

Baked Garlic Butter Cod

Prep Time: 5 minutes | Cook Time: 20 minutes | Serves 2

- Nonstick cooking spray, for coating the baking dish
- 2 garlic cloves
- 2 tablespoons unsalted butter, at room temperature
- 1 tablespoon olive oil
- 1/8 teaspoon paprika
- ¼ teaspoon table salt
- 1/8 teaspoon ground black pepper
- 1 tablespoon finely chopped fresh parsley
- 2 (4-ounce) cod fillets
- 1 lemon

1. Preheat the oven to 400°F. Spray a 9-by-9-inch baking dish with nonstick cooking spray.
2. Press each garlic clove so it gets a little squished, then peel off the papery layer and cut off the root ends (the nubby side). Mince the garlic: Moving the knife blade in a rocking motion, run the knife over the squished cloves repeatedly. Use the knife blade to turn the pile of cut garlic a quarter turn every few seconds. Continue this until the garlic is cut into very fine pieces (minced).
3. In a small bowl, using a spoon or even your fingers, combine the butter, olive oil, garlic, paprika, salt, pepper, and parsley. The mixture should resemble a paste.
4. Coat the entire outside of the cod fillets with the butter mixture and place them in a single layer in the prepared baking dish.
5. Cut the lemon into ¼-inch-thick slices. Place 2 slices on top of each piece of cod.
6. Lay the remaining slices around the bottom of the baking dish.
7. Transfer the baking dish to the oven and bake for 20 minutes, or until a meat thermometer inserted into the thickest part of the cod reads 145°F. Remove from the oven.
8. Drizzle the juices from the baking dish over the cod before serving.

Sticky Honey-Lime Salmon

Prep Time: 5 minutes | Cook Time: 10 minutes | Serves 4

- ¼ cup honey
- 3 tablespoons low-sodium soy sauce
- 1 tablespoon freshly squeezed lime juice
- 2 garlic cloves, minced
- 4 skinless salmon fillets
- Kosher salt
- Freshly ground black pepper
- 1 to 2 tablespoons olive oil
- Chopped scallions, for garnish (optional)

1. In a small bowl, whisk together the honey, soy sauce, lime juice, and garlic. Set aside.
2. Season the salmon fillets generously with salt and pepper. In a large nonstick sauté pan or skillet over medium-high heat, heat the olive oil until hot. Add the salmon and reduce the heat to medium. Cook for 3 to 4 minutes. Gently flip the fillets and cook for about 2 minutes more, until seared. Reduce the heat to low, and pour the sauce mixture onto the fillets. Continue to cook for 45 to 60 seconds, and gently flip the fillets to coat the other side in the sauce. Remove from the heat if necessary to allow the sauce to cool down (see Troubleshooting). Remove from the heat when the salmon is cooked to your liking. It should flake easily with a fork. Cook time will vary based on the thickness of the salmon fillets.
3. Transfer the fillets to a serving plate, reserving the sauce in the pan. Simmer the remaining sauce for another 30 to 60 seconds and spoon over the fillets. Garnish with scallions, if desired, and serve.

Fish Chowder

Prep Time: 5 minutes | Cook Time: 25 minutes | Serves 4 cups

- 1 (2-ounce, 1½-inch-thick) piece salt pork, cubed
- 1 small onion, coarsely chopped
- 1 cup water
- 2 potatoes, cut into 1¼-inch-long and ⅜-inch-thick strips
- 1 cup chicken broth
- 1 pound cod
- 2 cups milk
- ¼ teaspoon freshly ground black pepper
- 1 tablespoon butter

1. In a medium skillet over medium heat, sauté the salt pork until it's golden brown and crispy. Remove the pieces that are mostly pork (rather than mostly fat) from the skillet. To the salt-pork fat left in the skillet, add the onion and sauté for 7 minutes, until translucent.
2. In the same skillet over medium-high heat, bring the water to a boil. Once it's boiling, add the potato strips and continue boiling for 5 minutes. Add the chicken broth and cod and simmer uncovered for 10 minutes, or until the fish is done. Add the milk, pepper, and butter and heat until the butter melts.

Parsley Cod

Prep Time: 10 minutes | Cook Time: 15 minutes | Serves 4

- 3 tablespoons lemon juice
- 3 tablespoons butter, melted
- 1/4 cup all-purpose flour
- 1/2 teaspoon salt
- 1/4 teaspoon paprika
- 1/4 teaspoon lemon-pepper seasoning
- 4 (6 ounces) cod fillets
- 2 tablespoons minced fresh parsley
- 2 teaspoons grated lemon zest

1. At 400 degrees F, preheat your oven.
2. Mix lemon juice and butter in a shallow bowl.
3. Whisk flour with seasonings in another bowl.
4. Coat the fish with lemon juice mixture and coat with the flour mixture.
5. Place the coated fish in a casserole dish then pour the remaining lemon juice mixture on top.
6. Bake the fish for almost 15 minutes in the preheated oven.
7. Serve warm.

Easy Shrimp Scampi

Prep Time: 5 minutes | Cook Time: 20 minutes | Serves 2

- Salt, for cooking the linguine
- 1 (5-ounce) package linguine
- 1 onion
- 1 garlic clove
- 1 tablespoon unsalted butter, divided
- 1 tablespoon olive oil, divided
- Pinch red pepper flakes
- 1/3 pound large or extra-large shrimp, peeled and deveined
- ¼ teaspoon table salt
- 1/8 teaspoon ground black pepper
- ¼ cup chicken stock
- Juice of ½ lemon
- 2 tablespoons chopped fresh parsley

1. Bring a large pot of salted water to a boil over high heat.
2. Add the linguine and cook according to the package directions, usually about 10 minutes, until tender. Remove from the heat. Drain in a strainer.
3. To finely dice the onion, start by cutting the onion in half from root to tip. Peel off the papery outside layer and a layer of onion underneath that. For each onion half, cut off the tip of the onion, but leave the root end intact. Cut an onion half in half again from root to tip. Place an onion quarter, flat-side down, on a cutting board. Make several vertical cuts from end to end, being careful not to cut through the root end. Flip the onion quarter onto the other flat side and repeat the vertical cuts, again being careful not to cut through the root end. Then cut the onion crosswise into very fine, even dice—the pieces should just fall off the knife ready to go. Set aside ¼ cup and store any leftover onion.
4. Press the garlic clove so it gets a little squished, then peel off the papery layer and cut off the root end (the nubby side). Mince the garlic: Moving the knife blade in a rocking motion, run the knife over the squished clove repeatedly. Use the knife blade to turn the pile of cut garlic a quarter turn every few seconds. Continue this until the garlic is cut into very fine pieces (minced).
5. In a large skillet, heat ½ tablespoon of butter and ½ tablespoon of olive oil over medium-high heat until the butter has melted.
6. Add the onion, garlic, and red pepper flakes. Cook for 3 minutes, or until the onion is softened and translucent.
7. Add the chicken stock and lemon juice to the skillet. Bring to a simmer.
8. Add the remaining ½ tablespoon of butter and ½ tablespoon of olive oil. Whisk until combined and the butter has melted.
9. Add the cooked linguine.
10. Return the shrimp to the skillet, along with any juices that accumulated in the bowl. Using tongs, toss everything together.
11. Top the pasta with the parsley.

Cayenne Pepper Roasted Walnuts

Prep Time: 5 minutes | Cook Time: 15 minutes | Serves 4 cups

- 1 pound (454 g) walnut halves and pieces
- ½ cup granulated sugar
- 3 tablespoons vegetable oil
- 1 teaspoon cayenne pepper
- ½ teaspoon fine salt

1. Soak the walnuts in a large bowl with boiling water for a minute or two. Drain the walnuts. Stir in the sugar, oil and cayenne pepper to coat well. Spread the walnuts in a single layer on the sheet pan.
2. Select Roast. Set Air Fryer temperature to 325°F (163°C) and set time to 15 minutes. Press Start to begin preheating.
3. When the unit has preheated, place the pan into the oven.
4. After 7 or 8 minutes, remove the pan from the oven. Stir the nuts. Return the pan to the oven and continue cooking, check frequently.
5. When cooking is complete, the walnuts should be dark golden brown. Remove the pan from the oven. Sprinkle the nuts with the salt and let cool. Serve.

Rosemary Herbed Ricotta with Capers

Prep Time: 10 minutes | Cook Time: 8 minutes | Serves 4-6

- 1½ cups whole milk ricotta cheese
- 2 tablespoons extra-virgin olive oil
- 2 tablespoons capers, rinsed
- Zest of 1 lemon, plus more for garnish
- 1 teaspoon finely chopped fresh rosemary
- Pinch crushed red pepper flakes
- Salt and freshly ground black pepper, to taste
- 1 tablespoon grated Parmesan cheese

1. In a mixing bowl, stir together the ricotta cheese, olive oil, capers, lemon zest, rosemary, red pepper flakes, salt, and pepper until well combined.
2. Spread the mixture evenly in a baking dish.
3. Select Air Fry. Set Air Fryer temperature to 380°F (193°C) and set time to 8 minutes. Press Start to begin preheating. Once preheated, place the baking dish in the oven.
4. When cooking is complete, the top should be nicely browned. Remove from the oven and top with a sprinkle of grated Parmesan cheese. Garnish with the lemon zest and serve warm.

One-Pot Zucchini Mushroom Pasta

Prep Time: 10 minutes | Cook Time: 10 minutes | Serves 4-6

- 1 pound pasta
- 2 zucchinis, thinly sliced
- 1 pound cremini mushrooms, thinly sliced
- ⅔ cup peas
- 2 garlic cloves, minced
- ½ teaspoon dried thyme

- 4½ cups water
- ¼ cup heavy (whipping) cream
- ½ teaspoon salt
- ¼ teaspoon freshly ground black pepper
- ⅓ cup grated Parmesan cheese

1. In a large pot, combine the pasta, zucchini, mushrooms, peas, garlic, thyme, and water. Bring to a boil over medium-high heat. Reduce the heat to medium-low and simmer, uncovered, for 10 minutes, or until the noodles are al dente or done to your preference. Drain any excess water.
2. Stir in the cream, salt, pepper, and Parmesan. Serve.

Garden Salad

Prep Time: 10 minutes | Cook Time: 0 minutes | Serves 1

- 4 iceberg lettuce leaves
- ½ tomato
- 1 cucumber
- 2 celery stalks
- ½ cup sliced mushrooms
- ½ cup baby carrots
- 3 Tbsp low-calorie salad dressing, any flavor

1. Wash the lettuce leaves, tomato, cucumber, and celery stalks, and dice.
2. Wipe the mushrooms with a damp cloth.
3. Chop the baby carrots in half.
4. Combine all ingredients and toss with the salad dressing.

Spring Roll Salad

Prep Time: 20 minutes | Cook Time: 0 minutes | Serves 2

- 1 cup mung bean sprouts
- 1 carrot
- 2 English cucumbers, sliced diagonally
- 1 red bell pepper
- 1 (14-oz) can baby corn
- 2 tsp olive oil
- 3 tsp soy sauce
- 1 Tbsp red wine vinegar
- 1 tsp granulated sugar

1. Wash the vegetables. Drain the mung bean sprouts thoroughly.
2. Peel the carrot and cut into thin strips about 2 inches long.
3. Cut the red pepper in half, remove the seeds, and cut into thin strips about 2 inches long.
4. Rinse the baby corn in warm water and drain thoroughly.
5. Combine the olive oil, soy sauce, red wine vinegar, and sugar in a jar and shake well. Toss the salad with the dressing. Wait about 30 minutes to serve to allow the flavors to blend.

Spaghetti Marinara

Prep Time: 20 minutes | Cook Time: 40 minutes | Serves 6

- Kosher salt
- 1 pound spaghetti
- 3 tablespoons extra-virgin olive oil
- 4 cloves garlic, thinly sliced
- 1 small onion, finely chopped
- 1 teaspoon dried oregano
- 1 28-ounce can whole peeled tomatoes
- ½ cup chopped fresh basil
- 2 tablespoons unsalted butter, cut into cubes

1. ill a large pot with water and season with salt. Bring to a boil over high heat. Add the spaghetti and cook as the label directs for al dente. Carefully remove 1 cup of the pasta cooking water with a liquid measuring cup; set aside. Carefully drain the spaghetti in a colander set in the sink.
2. Meanwhile, heat the olive oil in a large skillet over medium heat. Add the garlic and cook until golden around the edges, about 3 minutes. Add the onion, oregano and 1 teaspoon salt. Cook, stirring with a wooden spoon, until the onion is soft but not browned, about 10 minutes. Empty the tomatoes into a bowl and crush with your hands. Add to the skillet along with ½ cup water; continue cooking until the sauce is slightly reduced, about 20 minutes. Stir in the basil and season with salt. Keep warm over low heat.
3. Add the spaghetti to the sauce along with the butter and ½ cup of the reserved cooking water. Increase the heat to medium and toss with tongs to coat, adding the remaining cooking water as needed to loosen the sauce. Use the tongs to serve the spaghetti.

Veggies and Rice Noodles with Peanut Sauce

Prep Time: 10 minutes | Cook Time: 20 minutes | Serves 4

- 1 (8-ounce) package pad thai brown rice noodles
- 1 (16-ounce) bag frozen stir-fry vegetables
- 5 tablespoons hot water, divided
- ¼ cup smooth peanut butter
- 2 tablespoons reduced-sodium soy sauce
- 1 tablespoon freshly squeezed lemon juice
- 1 teaspoon sriracha

1. Fill a stockpot with hot water and carefully place it over high heat. Bring to a boil. Add the rice noodles and cook according to the package instructions (this should take about 5 minutes). Place a colander in the sink and drain the noodles (but don't run them under cold water).
2. Pour the frozen vegetables into a large microwave-safe bowl with a lid (or use a microwave-safe plate to cover the bowl). Add 3 tablespoons of hot water to the vegetables. Cover the bowl and microwave for 8 minutes. Using a large slotted spoon, transfer the vegetables to another bowl, leaving any cooking water behind.
3. Meanwhile, in a large bowl, whisk the peanut butter, remaining 2 tablespoons of hot water, soy sauce, lemon juice, and sriracha until smooth; it will take a bit of stirring to get the peanut butter to blend in.
4. Using tongs, add the noodles and vegetables to the peanut butter sauce. Toss together to coat and combine. Serve hot.

Cheesy Bow Ties with Roasted Broccoli and Mozzarella Skewers

Prep Time: 30 minutes | Cook Time: 40 minutes | Serves 4

- Kosher salt
- 12 ounces bow tie pasta
- 1 small head broccoli, cut into florets
- 1 tablespoon extra-virgin olive oil, plus more for drizzling
- 3 tablespoons grated parmesan cheese
- 1 clove garlic, grated
- 2 tablespoons unsalted butter
- 3 tablespoons all-purpose flour
- 1½ cups milk
- ½ teaspoon dijon or yellow mustard
- 1½ cups shredded cheddar cheese
- Freshly ground pepper
- 8 mini mozzarella balls (bocconcini), halved
- 12 cherry tomatoes, halved

1. Preheat the oven to 450°. Fill a large pot with water and season with salt. Bring to a boil over high heat. Add the pasta and cook as the label directs for al dente. Carefully drain the pasta in a colander set in the sink. Reserve the pot.
2. Meanwhile, toss the broccoli on a baking sheet with 1 tablespoon olive oil, the parmesan and garlic. Carefully place in the oven and roast until the broccoli is slightly charred and the cheese starts browning, about 12 minutes.
3. Melt the butter in the reserved pasta pot over medium heat. Sprinkle in the flour and cook, whisking, until lightly toasted, about 2 minutes. Add the milk and mustard and cook, whisking occasionally, until thick and creamy, 4 to 5 minutes. Whisk in the cheddar and season with salt and pepper; continue cooking until the cheese is melted, 1 to 2 more minutes. Stir in the pasta until coated and warmed through, about 1 minute.
4. Thread the mozzarella and tomatoes onto 8 small skewers. Drizzle with olive oil and season with salt and pepper. Serve with the pasta and broccoli.

Savory Cabbage Slaw

Prep Time: 15 minutes plus 20 minutes to sit | Cook Time: 0 minutes | Serves 4

- 4 tablespoons olive oil
- 3 tablespoons fish sauce
- 1 tablespoon sherry vinegar
- Juice of 1 lime
- 1 teaspoon brown sugar
- Flake salt, such as Maldon
- ½ head red cabbage
- ½ head green cabbage
- Freshly ground black pepper

1. In a small bowl, combine the olive oil, fish sauce, vinegar, lime juice, sugar, and a small pinch of salt, whisking vigorously to dissolve the sugar. Taste, adjust seasoning as needed, and set aside.
2. With the flat side of the cabbage flush against your cutting board, use a very sharp knife to slice the cabbage very thinly and transfer to a large bowl. Use two forks to toss half the dressing in with the cabbage mix. Add the remainder, and toss again to coat. Season with pepper.
3. The slaw is best once the acids in the dressing soften the crunchy cabbage slightly, at least 20 minutes. Before serving, toss the slaw to reincorporate the dressing accumulated at the bottom of the bowl, then pile the slaw onto sandwiches or serve as a super-flavorful, crunchy side. Keeps in the refrigerator, covered, for 1 week.

Veggie Fried Rice

Prep Time: 10 minutes | Cook Time: 10 minutes | Serves 4

- 1 tablespoon sesame oil
- ½ cup chopped sweet onion
- ½ cup frozen peas and carrots
- 1 large egg, lightly beaten
- 1½ cups cooked rice
- 2 tablespoons soy sauce
- 3 tablespoons chopped scallions

1. In a large skillet or wok over medium-high heat, heat the oil. Once the oil is hot, add the onion and peas and carrots mixture, and cook for 4 to 5 minutes, or until tender.
2. Using a spatula, push the vegetable mixture to the side of the pan. Add the beaten egg, and scramble it in the pan. Once the egg is cooked through, mix the vegetables into the egg. Add the rice, stirring to incorporate. Add the soy sauce, and stir thoroughly, cooking until heated through.
3. Transfer the rice to a serving bowl, sprinkle the scallions over top, and serve.

Yummy Crispy Carrot Chips

Prep Time: 5 minutes | Cook Time: 20 minutes | Serves 6

- 4 to 5 medium carrots, trimmed and thinly sliced
- 1 tablespoon olive oil, plus more for greasing
- 1 teaspoon seasoned salt

1. Toss the carrot slices with 1 tablespoon of olive oil and salt in a medium bowl until thoroughly coated.
2. Grease the perforated pan with the olive oil. Place the carrot slices in the greased pan.
3. Select Air Fry. Set Air Fryer temperature to 390°F (199°C) and set time to 10 minutes. Press Start to begin preheating. Once preheated, place the pan into the oven. Stir the carrot slices halfway through the cooking time.
4. When cooking is complete, the chips should be crisp-tender. Remove the pan from the oven and allow cooling for 5 minutes before serving.

Asian Cucumber Salad

Prep Time: 10 minutes | Cook Time: 3 minutes | Serves 4

- 3 tablespoons rice wine vinegar
- 1 tablespoon toasted sesame oil
- 1 tablespoon soy sauce
- ½ teaspoon sugar
- 4 cups Persian, hothouse, or other thin-skinned cucumbers, scrubbed and chopped
- 2 scallions, ends trimmed and sliced thin on a diagonal
- ⅓ cup chopped fresh cilantro
- Pinch flake salt, such as Maldon
- 1 tablespoon sesame seeds

1. In a medium bowl, whisk to combine the rice wine vinegar, sesame oil, soy sauce, and sugar, dissolving the sugar.
2. Add the cucumbers, scallions, cilantro, and salt, and toss to coat well. Taste and adjust seasoning as necessary. Allow the salad to sit for at least 10 minutes for the flavors to meld.
3. In a small dry skillet over medium heat, toast the sesame seeds until golden, about 3 minutes.
4. Serve chilled with the toasted sesame seeds sprinkled on top. Pairs well with grilled meats, seared fish or shrimp, brown rice, or broiled, marinated tofu.

Pasta with Olive Oil, Garlic, and Romano Cheese

Prep Time: 5 minutes | Cook Time: 10 minutes | Serves 4

- ¾ cup extra-virgin olive oil
- 3 medium to large garlic cloves, finely chopped
- 1 (16-ounce) package spaghetti
- 1½ cups grated Romano cheese
- ½ teaspoon salt
- ¼ teaspoon freshly ground black pepper

1. Cook the pasta according to the package directions. Drain the pasta in a colander, and then transfer it to a large serving bowl.
2. Heat the olive oil in a medium skillet over medium heat. Add the garlic and cook for about 1 minute, just until it begins to turn golden and becomes fragrant. Pour the oil and garlic over the cooked pasta. Sprinkle it with the Romano cheese and toss. Season with salt and pepper.

Summery Corn And Watermelon Salad

Prep Time: 15 minutes | Cook Time: 0 minutes | Serves 4

- 5 fresh basil leaves
- ½ small watermelon, seeded, rind removed, cut into 1-inch cubes
- 2 ears fresh sweet corn, cooked and cut off cob
- 1 teaspoon ground sumac
- ¼ teaspoon ground cayenne
- Zest of ½ lemon
- Flake salt, such as Maldon

1. Transfer the cubed watermelon and any accumulated juices to a serving platter. Add the corn cut off the cobs (it is okay if there are rows of corn left intact; that is part of the fun). Sprinkle the sumac and cayenne over the mixture, followed by the lemon zest.
2. Do this immediately prior to serving the salad, as the edges of the basil will darken from being cut (known as oxidation). Stack the basil leaves on top of each other, and roll into a tight bundle. Slice your knife across the roll, creating very thin strips (called chiffonade). Fluff the chiffonade to separate the strips, and scatter onto the salad.
3. Season with salt, and serve immediately.

Tortellini & Spinach Soup

Prep Time: 5 minutes | Cook Time: 15 minutes | Serves 6

- 2 tablespoons olive or grapeseed oil
- 6 garlic cloves, minced
- 6 cups chicken broth
- 20 ounces packaged fresh cheese tortellini
- 1 (14.5-ounce) can crushed tomatoes
- 12 ounces baby spinach leaves
- Salt (optional)
- Freshly ground black pepper (optional)

1. In a Large Pot Over Medium-High Heat, Heat The Oil. Add The Garlic, And Sauté For 30 Seconds. Add The Broth, Increase The Heat To High, And Bring To a Boil.
2. Once The Broth Is Boiling, Add The Tortellini And Cook For Half The Cooking Time On The Package Directions. Add The Tomatoes, Reduce The Heat To Medium-Low, And Continue Cooking Until The Tortellini Is Tender.
3. Stir In The Spinach And Cook Until It Wilts, About a Minute. Season With Salt And Pepper, If Needed, Ladle Into Bowls, And Serve.

White Bean & Bacon Soup

Prep Time: 10 minutes | Cook Time: 40 minutes | Serves 4

- 6 slices bacon, chopped
- ½ cup diced onion
- ¼ cup diced carrot
- 3 garlic cloves, minced
- 1 tablespoon olive or grapeseed oil
- 2 (15-ounce) cans cannellini beans (white beans), drained and rinsed
- Dash kosher salt
- Dash freshly ground black pepper
- 2 cups (16 ounces) chicken stock

1. In a large pot over medium heat, cook the bacon until crisp, about 8 minutes. Scoop out the bacon, drain it on a paper towel–lined plate, and reserve the fat in the pot.
2. Add the onion and carrot and sauté in the bacon fat for 5 minutes. Add the garlic and sauté for 1 to 2 minutes, stirring frequently. Add the oil, then add the beans, salt, pepper, and chicken stock, stirring well to blend.
3. Reduce the heat to medium-low, and simmer for 25 minutes. Then, use a potato masher or the back of a wooden spoon to mash some of the beans to add creaminess to the soup. Turn off the heat and let the soup sit for at least 10 minutes. Ladle the soup into bowls, top each with bacon, and serve.

Chapter 8
Snacks and Drinks

Air Fried Garlic Tofu

Prep Time: 5 minutes | Cook Time: 13 minutes | Serves 3

- 8 ounces (227 g) firm tofu, pressed and cut into bite-sized cubes
- 1 tablespoon tamari sauce
- 1 teaspoon peanut oil
- ½ teaspoon garlic powder
- ½ teaspoon onion powder

1. Toss the tofu cubes with tamari sauce, peanut oil, garlic powder and onion powder.
2. Cook your tofu in the preheated Air Fryer at 380°F (193°C) for about 13 minutes, shaking the basket once or twice to ensure even browning. Enjoy!

Buttermilk Biscuit Apple Rolls

Prep Time: 5 minutes | Cook Time: 13 minutes | Serves 4

- 1 (10-ounce / 283-g) can buttermilk biscuits
- 1 apple, cored and chopped
- ¼ cup powdered sugar
- 1 teaspoon cinnamon
- 1 tablespoon coconut oil, melted

1. Line the bottom of the Air Fryer cooking basket with a parchment paper.
2. Separate the dough into biscuits and cut each of them into 2 layers. Mix the remaining ingredients in a bowl.
3. Divide the apple/cinnamon mixture between biscuits and roll them up. Brush the biscuits with coconut oil and transfer them to the Air Fryer cooking basket.
4. Cook the rolls at 330°F (166°C) for about 13 minutes, turning them over halfway through the cooking time. Enjoy!

Candied Grapes

Prep Time: 15 minutes | Cook Time: 35 minutes | Serves 4

- 1 3-ounce package grape gelatin powder
- 2 cups red seedless grapes

1. Sprinkle the gelatin powder on a rimmed baking sheet. Soak the grapes in a bowl of cold water. Remove a few of the grapes with a slotted spoon and put on the baking sheet; roll the grapes in the gelatin powder until coated. Place the coated grapes on a plate.
2. Repeat the process to coat the remaining grapes in small batches. Let dry, about 20 minutes.

Mini Quiches

Prep Time: 10 minutes | Cook Time: 15 minutes | Serves 24 quiches

- Butter, for greasing
- 4 whole eggs
- 1 egg yolk
- ⅓ cup heavy cream
- ¼ teaspoon freshly grated nutmeg
- Pinch ground cayenne pepper
- ½ teaspoon kosher salt (if you choose bacon, ham, or smoked fish as your "delicious addition," reduce to a pinch of salt instead)
- ½ teaspoon freshly ground black pepper
- ¾ cup shredded Gruyère cheese, divided

1. Preheat the oven to 375°F.
2. Grease a 24-cup mini muffin tin.
3. In a medium bowl, whisk together the eggs, yolk, cream, nutmeg, cayenne, salt, and pepper until frothy. Stir in ½ cup of shredded cheese.
4. Place the prepared muffin pan on a baking sheet to catch any drips. If you chose any delicious additions, add a teaspoonful to each cup. Transfer the egg mixture by ladling it into a measuring cup, and from there, pour the egg mixture into each cup, filling to just below the rim. The measuring cup's pour spout makes this a no-mess operation! Top the egg mixture with the remaining ¼ cup of shredded cheese, adding a small pinch to each quiche.
5. Bake until the tops are puffed and golden, 10 to 15 minutes. Let them cool for about 5 minutes.
6. Invert the tin over the baking sheet to pop out the quiches. Arrange them on a platter or individual plates, and serve.

Strawberries with Yogurt Dip

Prep Time: 5 minutes | Cook Time: 5 minutes | Serves 1

- 1 cup low-fat plain Greek yogurt
- 3 tablespoons strawberry preserves
- ¼ teaspoon pure vanilla extract
- ¼ teaspoon ground cinnamon
- 6 strawberries, stems removed

1. Put the yogurt in a small bowl. Add the strawberry preserves, vanilla and cinnamon and stir until swirled.
2. Thread the strawberries onto wooden skewers. Serve with the dip.

Mighty Meatballs

Prep Time: 20 minutes | Cook Time: 15 minutes | Serves 4

- 2 tablespoons buttermilk
- ¼ cup fresh bread crumbs
- 12 ounces ground beef
- ½ cup grated Parmesan cheese
- 2 pieces bacon, finely chopped
- Pinch freshly grated nutmeg
- 1 egg
- ⅓ cup chopped fresh parsley
- 2 garlic cloves, grated
- 2 tablespoons olive oil
- ¼ teaspoon Kosher salt
- ¼ teaspoon freshly ground black pepper

1. In a small bowl, add the buttermilk to the bread crumbs, and allow the crumbs to absorb the milk, 5 to 7 minutes. Meanwhile, put the ground beef in a medium bowl. Add the cheese, bacon, nutmeg, milk-soaked bread crumbs, egg, parsley, garlic, and olive oil to the meat, and sprinkle with salt and pepper. Overworking the mixture will produce tough, chewy meatballs, so mix everything just until combined.
2. Use 2 teaspoons to form the meat mixture into bite-size balls. Use the spoons to place them onto an aluminum-foil-lined baking sheet so that the heat of your hands doesn't warm them prior to cooking. Preheat the broiler with a rack in the topmost position.
3. Broil the meatballs until browned on top, checking them at about 5 minutes. Lower the heat to 350°F, and bake until tender and fully cooked, about 10 minutes.
4. Serve warm on a serving platter or plates.

Quick Pickles

Prep Time: 15 minutes | Cook Time: 5 minutes | Serves 3

- 4 or 5 large cucumbers, sliced thin
- 2 large red onions, sliced thin
- 3 cups white vinegar
- 1¾ cups sugar
- 1½ tablespoons kosher salt
- 1 tablespoon celery flakes
- 1 to 2 teaspoons red pepper flakes (depending how spicy you like it)
- 3 cups ice

1. In a large bowl, toss the sliced cucumbers and onions using tongs or 2 forks. Fill each jar with the vegetable mixture, using a spoon to gently push the veggies down to make room for more.
2. In a small pot, combine the vinegar, sugar, salt, celery flakes, and red pepper flakes, to taste. Bring to a boil. Remove the pot from the heat, and add the ice. Stir until the ice is melted. Fill the jars with the mixture just below the top.
3. Cover and allow the jars to cool to room temperature, then refrigerate until ready to enjoy.

Broccoli-Cheese Nuggets

Prep Time: 10 minutes | Cook Time: 20 minutes | Serves 8

- 1 teaspoon olive oil
- 2 eggs
- 2 garlic cloves
- 1 (16-ounce) package frozen broccoli, steamed
- ½ cup whole-wheat bread crumbs
- ½ cup shredded Cheddar cheese

1. Preheat the oven and crack the eggs. Preheat the oven to 400°F. Use your fingers or a paper towel to rub the olive oil all over a baking sheet. In a medium bowl, crack 1 egg. Remove any shells, and pour the egg into a large bowl. Repeat with the second egg. Beat the eggs with a whisk or fork until smooth.
2. Chop and mix the ingredients. Using a cutting board and a kid-safe knife, mince* the garlic. Chop the steamed broccoli into small pieces. Add the broccoli, bread crumbs, cheese, and garlic to the bowl with the eggs. Using a wooden spoon, mix well to combine.
3. Make the nuggets. Using your hands, take 1 tablespoon of the broccoli mixture and roll it into a ball or form it into a patty. Place it on the baking sheet. Repeat with the rest of the mixture, spreading all the nuggets out on the baking sheet.
4. Bake the nuggets. Bake in the oven for about 20 minutes, or until lightly brown and crispy on top. Cool and serve.

Sweet Plantain with Sorrel Spice Mix

Prep Time: 5 minutes | Cook Time: 10 minutes | Serves 2

- 1 very ripe, sweet plantain
- 1 teaspoon Caribbean Sorrel Rum Spice Mix
- 1 teaspoon coconut oil, melted

1. Cut your plantain into slices.
2. Toss your plantain with Caribbean Sorrel Rum Spice Mix and coconut oil.
3. Cook your plantain in the preheated Air Fryer at 400°F (204°C) for 10 minutes, shaking the cooking basket halfway through the cooking time.
4. Serve immediately and enjoy!

Strawberry-Lime Refrigerator Jam

Prep Time: 10 minutes | Cook Time: 15 minutes | Serves 12 ounces

- 2 pounds fresh strawberries, washed and hulled, diced small
- ¼ cup freshly squeezed lime juice
- 1½ cups sugar
- 1 tablespoon lime zest
- Pinch kosher salt

1. In a medium pot, combine all the ingredients. Mash the mixture with a potato masher.
2. Bring the mixture to a boil, stirring occasionally. Reduce the heat to medium-low and simmer for 15 minutes, stirring often. The mixture will foam up, but as it cooks down, it will calm down and thicken a little. Test for doneness by dipping a spoon or spatula in every so often. When it drips off the spoon in sections, remove from the heat.
3. Allow the mixture to cool completely. Refrigerate in a mason jar or covered glass bowl with a lid for up to 2 weeks.

Strawberry Fruit Leather

Prep Time: 20 minutes | Cook Time: 6 minutes | Serves 4

- 7 cups fresh strawberries

1. Line 2 baking sheets with parchment paper or silicone mat liners.
2. Place the strawberries onto a cutting board. Position a strawberry on its side and cut a V-shape into the top of the strawberry to cut out the stem. Repeat with all the strawberries.
3. Transfer the fruit to a blender or food processor. Cover with the lid and blend until the fruit is pureed. Divide the pureed fruit between the prepared baking sheets.
4. Place the baking sheets in the oven and bake for 6 to 8 hours, or until the middle is set and looks dry. Remove from the oven and let cool completely.
5. Using a pizza cutter, cut the cooled leather into strips or use cookie cutters to cut out fun shapes.

Cinnamon Applesauce

Prep Time: 10 minutes | Cook Time: 25 minutes | Serves 6

- 8 apples (4 each of 2 varieties, such as Golden Delicious, Pink Lady, Fuji, Gala, or Granny Smith), peeled, cored, and cut into 1-inch pieces
- 1½ cups water
- 3 tablespoons brown sugar
- 2 cinnamon sticks or 1 teaspoon ground cinnamon

1. In a medium pot, mix together all the ingredients. Cover and cook over medium heat for 20 to 25 minutes, or until the apples are cooked through (see Helpful Hints). Remove the mixture from the heat and allow to cool down for a few minutes.
2. Mash the apples.
3. With a potato masher or the back of a fork, mash the apples. Once mashed to your liking, allow to cool in the pot. Once cool, spoon the applesauce into a container or jars and refrigerate for up to a week.

Sparkling Orange Beverage

Prep Time: 1 hour 5 minutes | Cook Time: 0 minutes | Serves 10

- 2 cups simple syrup
- 2½ cups cold water
- 16 sprigs mint, chopped
- ¾ cup freshly squeezed orange juice
- 1 cup freshly squeezed lemon juice
- 4 tablespoons orange zest
- 2 liters ginger ale

1. In a 2-quart pitcher, combine the simple syrup, water, mint, orange juice, lemon juice, and orange zest. Stir to combine. Chill the juice mixture in the refrigerator for 1 hour, and then strain the liquid (I do this by putting a fine mesh strainer over a second pitcher and pouring from one pitcher into the other).
2. Fill 10 glasses halfway with ice, and then add 5 to 6 tablespoons of the juice mixture to each glass. Top off each glass with the ginger ale.

Grape Salsa

Prep Time: 15 minutes | Cook Time: 0 minutes | Serves 4

- 2 cups red and green grapes, quartered
- 2 tablespoons minced red onion
- 1 tablespoon minced fresh cilantro
- 2 tablespoons freshly squeezed lime juice
- 1 tablespoon honey
- ½ teaspoon red wine vinegar
- Pita chips or tortilla chips, for serving

1. In a small bowl, combine the grapes, onion, and cilantro, and toss to mix.
2. Combine the liquid ingredients and serve.
3. In a small jar with a lid, combine the lime juice, honey, and vinegar, and shake until it emulsifies. Pour the liquid over the salsa, and toss to coat. Serve with pita chips or tortilla chips.

Grape Rickey

Prep Time: 5 minutes | Cook Time: 5 minutes | Serves 8 cups

- 4 cups grape juice
- 6 tablespoons freshly squeezed lime juice
- 2 tablespoons powdered sugar
- 3½ cups lemon-lime soda
- Ice

1. Combine the fruit juices and the sugar, and then stir until the sugar dissolves. Add the soda.
2. Place ice in glasses and pour the Grape Rickey over the ice to serve.

Chunky Guacamole

Prep Time: 10 minutes | Cook Time: 10 minutes | Serves 3

- ½ small onion, chopped
- ½ teaspoon chopped jalapeño
- 3 ripe tomatoes, cored and chopped
- 1 garlic clove, peeled and chopped
- ½ tablespoon chopped cilantro
- 3 ripe avocados
- ½ teaspoon salt
- ¼ teaspoon freshly ground black pepper
- 1 tablespoon freshly squeezed lime juice

1. In a bowl, combine the onion, jalapeño, tomato, garlic, and cilantro.
2. Halve the avocados lengthwise and scoop out and discard the pits. Scrape the pulp of the avocado from the skin and add it to the bowl with the tomato mixture. Using a fork, mash the avocado while mixing it with the other ingredients, making a thick, chunky mass. Season with salt and pepper, add the lime juice, and stir to blend.
3. Cover the mixture with plastic wrap and place it in the refrigerator, allowing the flavors to blend for at least 5 minutes before serving.

Spinach Dip

Prep Time: 10 minutes | Cook Time: 25 minutes | Serves 6

- 3 pounds frozen chopped spinach, thawed and drained
- 1 pound cream cheese
- 4 cups shredded cheese (I recommend a mix of Monterey jack and mozzarella)
- 2 teaspoons hot cayenne powder
- ½ cup breadcrumbs

1. Preheat the oven to 350°F.
2. Place the spinach, cream cheese, shredded cheese, and cayenne in a bowl. Using an electric hand mixer, or by hand, mix the ingredients in the bowl until well blended. Transfer the mixture to a 13-by-9-inch pan and sprinkle the breadcrumbs on top.
3. Place the pan on the center rack in the preheated oven. Bake for 25 minutes, or until bubbly. Refrigerate any unused dip. It will keep for 3 to 4 days.

Cheddar Biscuits

Prep Time: 30 minutes | Cook Time: 45 minutes | Serves 10

- 2 cups of biscuit mix
- A quarter cup of butter
- 2/3 of a cup of milk
- A single cup of mild cheddar cheese that is shredded
- A quarter teaspoon of garlic powder

1. Heat your oven to 450 F.
2. Grease a baking sheet.
3. Mix the biscuit mix, milk, and cheese in a bowl. Make sure that the batter is doughy and soft. A wooden spoon will help with this, and it should take half a minute.
4. Put the batter on the sheet in spoonfuls.
5. Bake 10 minutes, and the biscuits should be a light brown.
6. Heat the garlic and butter in a pan on low heat until it is melted. This will take 5 minutes.
7. Brush that mix over the biscuits.

Lemon Raspberry Muffins

Prep Time: 24 minutes | Cook Time: 60 minutes | Serves 12

- Half a cup of honey
- 2 eggs
- A single cup of plain Greek yogurt
- A single cup and ¾ of white whole wheat flour
- A single teaspoon of baking powder
- Half a teaspoon of baking soda
- A third of a cup of coconut oil that is melted
- 2 teaspoons of vanilla extract
- The zest from a lemon
- A single cup and a half of organic raspberries
- A single tablespoon of turbinado sugar

1. Heat your oven to 350 F.
2. Grease a 12-cup muffin tin with coconut oil or cooking spray.
3. Get a large bowl. Combine flour, baking soda, baking powder, and blend with a whisk. Get another bowl and combine the honey oil, and beat them together with a whisk.
4. Add in the eggs and beat them well before adding the zest, vanilla, and yogurt. Mix it all well. If the oil gets solid, microwave it for half a minute. Pour your wet Ingredients into the dry. Mix it with a large spoon until it has just combined.
5. Fold raspberries in the batter. It will be thick. Divided into 12 cups and add sugar to the top. Bake 24 minutes and the toothpick should come out clean.
6. Let cool on a cooling rack.

Pizza Pockets

Prep Time: 15 minutes | Cook Time: 40 minutes | Serves 4

- A third of a cup of Parmesan that is grated
- A quarter of a cup of Parmesan that is grated
- 8 ounces of turkey sausage (Italian)
- A single tablespoon of olive oil
- A single beaten egg
- A single cup and a half of marinara sauce
- All-purpose flour
- A single pizza crust store-bought
- 4 ounces of room temperature cream cheese
- A cup of arugula tightly packed

1. Heat your olive oil over a heat that is medium-high and in a medium heavy skillet.
2. Add in the sausage and cook until it is golden and crumbled. 5 minutes. Add the arugula and cook it until it has wilted. Turn off your heat and let it cool for 19 minutes. Add in your cream cheese and a third of the parmesan. Stir, so it combines.
3. Preheat your oven to 400 F. Roll out your dough and make a big rectangle. Cut it in half.
4. Do this again until you have eight equal rectangles. Put your toppings onto one of the sides of each rectangle. Brush the edges with egg wash. Close the rectangle of dough over the topping. Use a fork to seal them up.
5. Put the pockets on the baking sheet that is lined with parchment paper. Brush the tops with egg wash. Sprinkle the rest of the cheese on top. Bake for 15 minutes. Heat your marinara sauce over low heat. Serve with sauce when done.

Cherry-Peach Twin Pops

Prep Time: 15 minutes | Cook Time: 15 minutes plus 4 hours freezing | Serves 6

- 1½ cups sour-cherry juice or nectar
- 3 tablespoons superfine sugar
- 1½ cups peach nectar

1. Combine the cherry juice and sugar in a large bowl and whisk until the sugar dissolves. Pour half of the cherry juice mixture into 3 or 4 ice pop molds, filling them to different heights. Pour half of the peach nectar into 3 or 4 more pop molds, filling them to different heights. Freeze until firm, about 2 hours.
2. Fill the cherry pops with the remaining peach nectar and fill the peach pops with the remaining cherry juice mixture. Insert wooden sticks into the pops and freeze until firm, at least 2 hours or overnight. To release the pops, run the molds under warm water.

Ice Cream Sundae Cones

Prep Time: 30minutes | Cook Time: 40 minutes plus 3 hours freezing | Serves 6

- 6 waffle cones
- 1 cup malted milk balls, plus 6 more for the cones
- 4 large chocolate-covered peanut butter cups
- 2 quarts vanilla and/or chocolate ice cream
- ¼ cup chocolate fudge sauce
- 1 7-ounce bottle chocolate shell topping
- ½ cup roasted peanuts, finely chopped

1. Place a stainless-steel bowl in the freezer for 20 minutes. Meanwhile, set 6 tall glasses on a baking sheet and put a waffle cone in each (the glasses will keep the cones upright). Drop 1 malted milk ball into each cone.
2. Roughly chop the remaining malted milk balls and the peanut butter cups with a chef's knife and put in the cold bowl. Add the ice cream. Smash and stir the candies into the ice cream with a metal spoon, working quickly to keep it from melting.
3. Press 1 small scoop of the ice cream into each cone. Spoon a heaping teaspoon of fudge sauce on top, then top with 2 generous scoops of the ice cream. Freeze the cones (in the glasses) until firm, about 2 hours.
4. Pour the chocolate shell topping into a bowl. Remove the cones from the glasses and dip the ice cream in the chocolate shell, swirling to coat. Immediately sprinkle the peanuts over the chocolate and place the cones upright in the glasses. Freeze until the chocolate shell is set, at least 1 hour or overnight.

Blueberry Pound Cake

Prep Time: 45 minutes | Cook Time: 1 hour 30 minutes | Serves 10

- 2 Tablespoons of butter
- A quarter cup of white sugar
- 2 ¾ cups of all-purpose flour
- A single teaspoon of baking powder
- A single cup of butter
- 4 eggs
- 2 cups of white sugar
- 2 cups of blueberries that are fresh
- A single teaspoon of vanilla extract
- A quarter cup of flour that is all-purpose

1. Preheat your oven to 325 F. Grease a pan that is 10 inches with 2 tablespoons of butter.
2. Sprinkle that same pan with a quarter cup of sugar. Mix 2 ¾ of the cup of flour with the baking powder and place it to the side.
3. Get a bowl and cream a cup of butter and 2 cups of sugar together until it has become fluffy and light. Beat the eggs one at a time before stirring the vanilla in. Slowly beat in your flour mix. Dredge your berries with the last quarter cup of flour.
4. Fold into the batter before pouring it into your

prepared pan. Bake for 80 minutes. The toothpick test should show a clean toothpick.
5. Let cool for 10 minutes into the pan before letting it cool on a wire rack.

Peach-Blueberry Crisp

Prep Time: 10 minutes | Cook Time: 45 minutes | Serves 4

- ⅔ cup rolled oats
- ⅓ cup packed brown sugar, plus 3 tablespoons for fruit
- ¼ cup plus 2 tablespoons all-purpose flour, divided
- ½ teaspoon ground cinnamon
- 2 teaspoons fresh ginger, finely grated Kosher salt
- ¾ stick butter, freezer-cold and cubed
- 2 pounds peaches or nectarines, cut into thin wedges
- 2 cups blueberries
- 2 teaspoons freshly squeezed lemon juice
- 1 teaspoon lemon zest

1. In a large bowl, stir with a fork to combine the oats, ⅓ cup of brown sugar, ¼ cup plus 1 tablespoon of flour, and the cinnamon. Add the ginger, a pinch of salt, and the butter to the mixture, and work the butter into the dry ingredients with your fingers until pea-size crumbs remain. Refrigerate.
2. Preheat the oven to 375°F.
3. In another large bowl, stir together the peaches and blueberries with the lemon juice and zest, the remaining 3 tablespoons of brown sugar, the remaining tablespoon of flour, and a pinch of salt. Toss all to combine.
4. Pour the fruit mixture into a baking dish, then spoon the oat mixture on top to coat. On a baking sheet, bake the crisp until the topping is golden and the juices bubble, 30 to 45 minutes. Allow the crisp to cool on a wire cooling rack for at least 20 minutes.
5. The crisp is delicious served warm, room temp, or even cold. It's so virtuous you could even eat it for breakfast! This fruity number is excellent all by itself, but it would be amazing topped with ice cream.

Frozen Yogurt Banana Pops

Prep Time: 15 minutes | Cook Time: 30 minutes plus 3 hours freezing | Serves 8

- 2 bananas
- Strawberry yogurt, for dipping
- Sliced nuts, granola, shredded coconut, and/or crushed freeze-dried fruit, for sprinkling

1. Cut the bananas in half crosswise with a chef's knife, then cut each in half lengthwise. Insert a wooden stick into the bottom of each. Put on a baking sheet and freeze until firm, about 3 hours.
2. Dip each banana in yogurt to coat and sprinkle with nuts, granola, coconut and/or freeze-dried fruit. Return to the baking sheet and freeze until set, about 10 minutes.

Dreamy Cheesecake

Prep Time: 20 minutes plus 3 hours to chill | Cook Time: 10 minutes | Serves 10

- 1 packet whole wheat graham crackers (9 crackers)
- 1 teaspoon ground cinnamon
- 3 tablespoons cane sugar
- ½ teaspoon kosher salt
- ⅓ cup butter, melted
- 2 (8-ounce) packages cream cheese, at room temperature
- ¼ teaspoon pure vanilla extract
- 1 teaspoon finely grated lemon zest
- 1¼ cups cane sugar
- 2 tablespoons all-purpose flour
- ¼ teaspoon kosher salt
- 5 whole eggs, plus 1 egg yolk
- ¼ cup heavy cream

1. Put the graham crackers in a resealable plastic bag. With a rolling pin, crush the crackers into crumbs. If you prefer a finer crust, continue crushing the crackers until you've reached a texture you like. In a medium bowl, mix together the crushed graham crackers, cinnamon, sugar, and salt. Pour in the melted butter, and stir to combine.
2. Use a rubber spatula or the back of a spoon to spread and compress the mixture evenly into a 9-inch springform pan. Press the crust a little up the sides of the pan, ensuring the crust is even at its base and thins as it goes up. Chill in the refrigerator to set while you make the filling.
3. Preheat the oven to 500°F.
4. In a large bowl, beat the cheese with an electric mixer until fluffy. Add the vanilla and lemon zest, and mix to combine.
5. In a small bowl, stir together the sugar, flour, and salt. Gradually blend the dry ingredients into the cheese. One at a time, add the eggs and additional yolk, whipping to combine and pausing after each to scrape down the sides of the bowl. Gently incorporate the cream, and whip to combine.
6. Pour the mixture into the crust. Place on a baking sheet, and bake for 5 to 8 minutes. Lower the temperature to 200°F, and bake for about 45 to 55 minutes more, until the edges are golden and the center still jiggles. Turn the oven off, and with the door ajar, allow the cheesecake to cool inside for about an hour. Refrigerate for 3 hours, up to overnight.
7. Remove the cake from the refrigerator. Run a butter knife around the inside edge to loosen the cake from the pan. Open the springform pan, remove the cake, and serve at once.

Chocolate-Pomegranate Brownies

Prep Time: 10 minutes | Cook Time: 30 minutes | Serves 12

- 12 ounces semisweet dark chocolate (such as Callebaut), chopped, divided
- 1½ sticks butter, cut into cubes
- 4 eggs
- 1¼ cup light brown sugar
- 1 cup all-purpose flour
- Seeds from ½ fresh pomegranate, for topping

1. Preheat the oven to 350°F.
2. Using a double boiler, melt half the chocolate and all the butter. Be careful that the water doesn't bubble up into the top saucepan as you do so, or it will ruin the chocolate. Remove the melted chocolate pan from the hot water bath, wipe the base with a dry dish towel to ensure no drips, stir the butter-chocolate mixture together, and set aside.
3. Line a square or small rectangular baking dish with parchment long enough that the paper extends beyond edges by at least 2 inches on all sides.
4. In a large bowl, use a fork or hand mixer to thoroughly combine the eggs, sugar, and flour. Add the slightly cooled, melted chocolate mixture and the remaining portion of chopped chocolate, stirring to combine.
5. Pour the mixture into the prepared baking dish, and bake for 25 minutes, or until a skewer or toothpick comes out almost clean. If you jiggle the tin, the center should move just a little.
6. Cool the brownies on a wire cooling rack for 10 minutes in the pan; then, using the parchment tabs on either side, lift the brownies out.
7. Cut the brownies into squares, and scatter the pomegranate seeds on top. Enjoy the delicious combo of still-molten chocolate and tart, juicy pomegranate!

Caramel Apple Nachos

Prep Time: 15 minutes | Cook Time: 0 minutes | Serves 4

- 2 apples
- 2 pears
- ¼ cup prepared caramel sauce (heated in the microwave according to the package instructions, if you like)
- 2 tablespoons sweetened shredded coconut
- 2 tablespoons mini semisweet chocolate chips
- Crushed pretzels, for topping (optional)
- Granola, for topping (optional)
- Dried fruit, for topping (optional)

1. On a cutting board, use an apple corer to core the apples. Cut the apples and pears into slices. Arrange the fruit slices on a serving platter.
2. Drizzle the fruit with the caramel sauce.
3. Sprinkle the caramel with coconut, chocolate chips, and other toppings, as desired. Enjoy.

Croissants

Prep Time: 45 minutes | Cook Time: 60 minutes | Serves 12

- A single cup of milk
- 4 cups of flour that is all-purpose
- A third of a cup of sugar that is granulated
- 2 and a quarter teaspoon of salt that is kosher
- 4 teaspoons of yeast that is active and dry
- A cup and a quarter of butter that is cold and unsalted
- An egg wash (this is to have a single large egg, and you beat it with a teaspoon of water)

1. Place your yeast and salt along with the flour and sugar in a bowl and whisk it all together until it has combined well. Slice your butter into slices an eighth of an inch thick and toss it into the flour mix so that the butter is coated.
2. Add your milk in and stir it together. A stiff dough will be made. Wrap your dough and make sure it's tight. You are going to use plastic wrap. Let it chill for 60 minutes.
3. Get yourself a lightly floured surface and roll your dough into a big and long rectangle.
4. Fold and make it like a letter. This means you fold it into thirds. Turn it 90 degrees and repeat 4 times. The dough should be flat and smooth with streaks of butter in it.
5. Rewrap it again and chill for another 60 minutes. Divide the dough in half and then roll again. It should be an eighth of an inch thick. Cut your dough into triangles that are long and skinny. Notch your wide end of each triangle you made with a half-inch cut.
6. Roll from the wide end to the end with a point. Tuck the point under the croissant.
7. Place on a baking sheet that is lined with parchment. Cover with plastic wrap (loosely) and allow it to proof for 120 minutes. Preheat your oven to 375 F. Brush the croissants with your egg wash. Bake 20 minutes. They should be a puffy brown golden color, and they should be flaky.

Flognarde (Apple-Custard Bake)

Prep Time: 15 minutes | Cook Time: 30 minutes | Serves 4

- 4 tablespoons butter, cubed, plus more for greasing the pan
- 5 tablespoons flour
- 4 tablespoons sugar
- Zest of 2 Meyer lemons
- ⅔ cup whole milk
- 4 eggs
- 3 apples, peeled, cored, and cut into ½-inch wedges
- Confectioners' sugar, for dusting

1. Butter a cast-iron skillet.
2. Preheat the oven to 400°F.
3. In a medium bowl, mix together the flour, sugar, lemon zest, and milk. Add the eggs and beat vigorously. Continue whisking as you pour the mixture into the pan.
4. Fan the apple wedges and lay them onto the mixture. It's okay if they slide a little as you arrange them.
5. Dot the surface with butter, and bake until the custard puffs and has turned golden brown at the edges, about 30 minutes.
6. Dust confectioners' sugar onto the custard. Serve hot or at room temperature, cut into wedges.

Chocolate and Fruit Cones

Prep Time: 30 minutes | Cook Time: 0 minutes | Serves 12

- ½ cup semisweet chocolate chips
- ½ cup butterscotch chips
- 12 sugar or waffle cones
- 1 (16-ounce) carton fresh strawberries, tops removed, sliced
- 1 large bunch seedless grapes
- 1 (12-ounce) carton fresh blueberries

1. Line a clean work surface with parchment paper.
2. In a medium microwave-safe bowl, combine the chocolate chips and butterscotch chips. Microwave on high power for 1 minute. Carefully remove the bowl from the microwave and stir the chips. Continue to microwave in 20-second increments, stirring between each, until the chips are melted.
3. Dip the top of a waffle cone into the melted chocolate and butterscotch chips, and place the dipped cone on the parchment paper to set. Repeat with the remaining cones.
4. In a medium bowl, gently stir together the strawberries, grapes, and blueberries.
5. Once the coating has set on the cones (this should take about 15 minutes), spoon fruit into each cone and serve.

Banana-Berry Split

Prep Time: 10 minutes | Cook Time: 0 minutes | Serves 4

- 4 bananas
- 16 ounces vanilla yogurt, divided
- ½ cup chocolate chips or chocolate shavings
- 1 cup blueberries or your favorite berry
- Chocolate sauce or caramel sauce, for drizzling
- Multicolored sprinkles/jimmies, for garnish

1. Peel the bananas and halve them lengthwise. In each of 4 bowls, position 2 banana halves side by side, spoon ½ cup of the yogurt over top of each, and sprinkle each with the chocolate chips and berries.
2. Drizzle with chocolate and/or caramel sauce, dust with colorful sprinkles/jimmies, and serve.

Froyo Dots

Prep Time: 15 minutes plus 30 minutes to freeze | Cook Time: 0 minutes | Serves 2-4

- ½ cup flavored yogurt of choice
- ¼ cup cream cheese, at room temperature
- 2 tablespoons powdered sugar

1. Line a Large Baking Sheet With Parchment Paper.
2. In a Medium Bowl, Combine The Yogurt, Cream Cheese, And Powdered Sugar. Using a Hand Mixer, Mix Until All Is Well Combined.
3. Using a Spatula, Transfer The Mixture To a Resealable Bag, Press The Air Out, And Seal The Bag Shut. Twist The Top Of The Bag, Pushing The Mixture To The Bottom Of The Bag, And Hold The Bag Firmly. Snip a Little Bit Off a Bottom Corner Of The Bag, Creating a Piping Bag. Gently Squeeze The Piping Bag, Piping Dots That Are About ¼ Inch Wide Onto The Parchment. Continue Piping Dots Until The Mixture Is Used Up, Covering The Parchment. (Depending On The Size Of Your Dots, This Recipe Makes About 50 Dots.)
4. Transfer The Baking Sheet To The Freezer And Freeze For 30 Minutes. Using Your Hands Or a Flipper, Remove The Dots From The Parchment. Serve In Bowls Or Store In a Resealable Bag In The Freezer.

Watermelon-Lime Sorbet

Prep Time: 10 minutes plus 6 hours to freeze | Cook Time: 1 minute | Serves 6

- 6 cups cubed watermelon
- ¼ cup water
- 3 tablespoons sugar
- ¼ cup freshly squeezed lime juice (2 to 3 limes)

1. Line a baking sheet with parchment paper or wax paper. Spread the watermelon cubes on the baking sheet, and freeze for 30 minutes. Transfer the cubes to a freezer-safe container in the freezer for at least 6 hours or overnight.
2. When ready to make the sorbet, make a simple syrup by heating the water and sugar in a small pot over medium heat and stirring. Once the sugar is dissolved, remove from the heat. Place the frozen watermelon and lime juice in a food processor or high-powered blender, drizzle in the warm simple syrup, and blend until the watermelon breaks down into an icy slush. Enjoy immediately or freeze for 30 minutes.

Appendix 1 Measurement Conversion Chart

Volume Equivalents (Dry)

US STANDARD	METRIC (APPROXIMATE)
1/8 teaspoon	0.5 mL
1/4 teaspoon	1 mL
1/2 teaspoon	2 mL
3/4 teaspoon	4 mL
1 teaspoon	5 mL
1 tablespoon	15 mL
1/4 cup	59 mL
1/2 cup	118 mL
3/4 cup	177 mL
1 cup	235 mL
2 cups	475 mL
3 cups	700 mL
4 cups	1 L

Volume Equivalents (Liquid)

US STANDARD	US STANDARD (OUNCES)	METRIC (APPROXIMATE)
2 tablespoons	1 fl.oz.	30 mL
1/4 cup	2 fl.oz.	60 mL
1/2 cup	4 fl.oz.	120 mL
1 cup	8 fl.oz.	240 mL
1 1/2 cup	12 fl.oz.	355 mL
2 cups or 1 pint	16 fl.oz.	475 mL
4 cups or 1 quart	32 fl.oz.	1 L
1 gallon	128 fl.oz.	4 L

Temperatures Equivalents

FAHRENHEIT(F)	CELSIUS(C) APPROXIMATE)
225 °F	107 °C
250 °F	120 ° °C
275 °F	135 °C
300 °F	150 °C
325 °F	160 °C
350 °F	180 °C
375 °F	190 °C
400 °F	205 °C
425 °F	220 °C
450 °F	235 °C
475 °F	245 °C
500 °F	260 °C

Weight Equivalents

US STANDARD	METRIC (APPROXIMATE)
1 ounce	28 g
2 ounces	57 g
5 ounces	142 g
10 ounces	284 g
15 ounces	425 g
16 ounces (1 pound)	455 g
1.5 pounds	680 g
2 pounds	907 g

Appendix 2 The Dirty Dozen and Clean Fifteen

The Environmental Working Group (EWG) is a nonprofit, nonpartisan organization dedicated to protecting human health and the environment Its mission is to empower people to live healthier lives in a healthier environment. This organization publishes an annual list of the twelve kinds of produce, in sequence, that have the highest amount of pesticide residue-the Dirty Dozen-as well as a list of the fifteen kinds ofproduce that have the least amount of pesticide residue-the Clean Fifteen.

THE DIRTY DOZEN	
The 2016 Dirty Dozen includes the following produce. These are considered among the year's most important produce to buy organic:	
Strawberries	Spinach
Apples	Tomatoes
Nectarines	Bell peppers
Peaches	Cherry tomatoes
Celery	Cucumbers
Grapes	Kale/collard greens
Cherries	Hot peppers

The Dirty Dozen list contains two additional itemskale/collard greens and hot peppers-because they tend to contain trace levels of highly hazardous pesticides.

THE CLEAN FIFTEEN	
The least critical to buy organically are the Clean Fifteen list. The following are on the 2016 list:	
Avocados	Papayas
Corn	Kiw
Pineapples	Eggplant
Cabbage	Honeydew
Sweet peas	Grapefruit
Onions	Cantaloupe
Asparagus	Cauliflower
Mangos	

Some of the sweet corn sold in the United States are made from genetically engineered (GE) seedstock. Buy organic varieties of these crops to avoid GE produce.

Appendix 3 Index

FRANCISCA W. CHILDS